DEALING WITH ADDICTION
WHY THE 20TH CENTURY WAS WRONG

DEALING WITH ADDICTION
WHY THE 20TH CENTURY WAS WRONG

Peter Ferentzy PhD Crackhead

Copyright 2011 Peter Ferentzy PhD Crackhead

ISBN 978-1-105-00410-0

Cover photo by: Noel Chris Miller

Contents

Why I wrote this book vii

Introduction xi

1. "You need to hit bottom"—a myth that kills 1
2. Abstinence is the only realistic solution—biggest lie in the business 9
3. Treatment produces abstinence—the second biggest lie 15
4. "All I have to share is my own experience"—your experience might not mean what you think it does 27
5. Codependency—a stupid word that doesn't mean anything 35
6. "Don't enable the addict"—why not? It's really the only solution 39
7. How this nonsense all started—a bit of history that everyone should know 43
8. The meaning of addiction—there's more to it than dependence 51
9. Recovery from addiction—time to get serious about what that means 55
10. Odds and ends—things that we can do without 61
11. Postscript 75
12. Further reading 77

Why I wrote this book

My name is Peter. I work in the addiction field, and I'm also a recovering crack addict. Yeah, alcoholic too, but it was crack that took me down. For real: I liked being an alcoholic, but a crack addiction on top of that made things hard to juggle. A few drinks would lead to a three-day run. On this point I'm not alone: crack really screwed up my alcoholism. A shame really, but there's no going back.

Unlike most recovering druggies in the addiction business, I don't work in treatment or any kind of counseling. I'm a research scientist, a Ph.D. Just go to my website and you'll see much of what I've been up to (http://www.peterferentzy.com). Unlike most of the recovering people on the frontlines, addicts in the drug scene, or those in the 12 Step world, I actually understand what's going on. That's not a joke, and it's not a boast—just the truth.

Throughout this book, I attempt to convey just that. I do my best to keep it free of specialized jargon or intricate logical points. But I'm not here to talk down to my readers: titles of scientific and other books and articles are offered to anyone wanting to pursue these matters further. This is not the type of manuscript where points made are accompanied by references, and then backed by numerous points and counterpoints. That kind of scholarly detail and precision would entail that each chapter be almost a book on its own. I want to keep this book brief and accessible—and I strongly urge my readers to make use of the sources provided at the end. Knowledge is power. So read, learn, educate yourself!

Why did I write this book? I'm sick of seeing people suffer needlessly, and die needlessly. The assumptions upon which the North American approach to addiction has been based since the early 20th century are mistaken, nasty, and stupid—when it comes right down to it, they amount to genocide.

But I've known this for almost 20 years, so why am I writing this book now?

As I write these words, it is November 16, 2010. Last December, a woman I knew—just a friend—OD'd in my home. She had sworn to me that she was clean, and I told her that she had better not bring any pipes or needles into my apartment. "I won't check your purse," I said, "and I won't hit a chick—but if I give you a noogie, you'll wish I was hitting you!" Ha, ha. She was over for the weekend to connect with her eight-year-old boy who lived in town with his dad. That Saturday we saw the kid, went to a community center, played, and had fun. Then we dropped off the boy, had dinner with my mom, and went back to my place. Everything seemed cool, but I woke up at midnight to find her body in the washroom, naked and cold.

You see, she had been in pain and was taking meds legitimately for that. She was supposed to take them orally. But she was always more likely to shoot up when not on methadone. She'd smash now and then anyway, but it would become daily—and far less controlled—when she wasn't on the methadone. People, including preachy do-gooders in the treatment system, had convinced her that methadone maintenance was still "using," that a reduction in frequency and intensity of injections is not a "real" answer. No matter how painful, they said, it's best to do it absolutely clean—all or nothing. She bought it and really tried. Can I ever prove that her death would not have occurred had she been on the methadone? Of course not. But we were very close. I used to get high with her, and I understood her patterns as well as anyone. There's no doubt in my mind.

At the funeral, I barely had the pluck to look her kid in the eye. What's there to say?

I remember thinking: this woman was never a menace to society, just a pain in the ass—little monkey would bump into a telephone pole, then blame the city for putting it there. Yet she was treated like someone who should be made to suffer—and suffer horribly—because somehow that would do her good.

But there's no reason for any of this—none! And this book will tell you why.

Only a few months back, I saw another one die. The hospital was kind enough to let me know that life support was to be withdrawn so that I could see her off. She had OD'd shooting crack over a month prior. Not good to shoot that. It tends to be dirty, and it's worse when scraped off a used pipe screen. Paralysis set in, among other things. Though I saw her almost every day for a month, there was no family in sight. She'd have died alone had I not been there.

By then, she was in a coma. Hoping that she could hear me, I whispered that I love her, and that her nightmare is over. When she went under, I cried like a baby. Outside the hospital, I hurled a string of profanities at the heavens.

You see, she had been doing a hit-and-miss job of cutting down on her drug use—stopping now and then, slowing down where possible. Some frontline person—a recovering addict—had told her that such efforts are a waste of time: if you can't kick, all that stopping and starting—all those efforts to slow down—will do no good at all. She took that to heart, and gave up trying.

But that frontline person was wrong, and is now responsible for my friend's death. In a better world, that individual would also be legally accountable. This book will tell you why.

So why am I writing this book? The 20th century approach to addictions, including alcoholism, has largely been governed by ideas and practices that simply add to the damage. No matter what the system—which includes the 12 Step movement—tries to feed you, it all has to change.

Why am I writing this book? Maybe it's because I believe that, someday soon, anyone on the frontlines who talks the kind of nonsense that killed my friends will face justice, or at least lose their professional standing. I've long understood that those who tell addicts that they need to hit bottom are accomplices to an abomination. I also knew that most of them had been snowed into believing that they're doing good. So for a long time my attitude was similar to that of a man who, long ago, said that such people should be forgiven, "for they know not what they do." But I've changed. Through it all, the people feeding so many lies and half-truths—to addicts, to alcoholics, to the general public—made a mistake. A really big one, too: they pissed me off.

Introduction

Some people get upset because I call myself "crackhead." Well, here's something I learned from Ice-T some 20 years ago: call yourself what really fits. Look at the situation, and expose sugarcoated lingo for the bullshit that it is. Anyone who doesn't want to be called crackhead can call himself a "person of crack" for all I care.

I've been studying addiction-related matters for over 20 years, but this book was written in such a way that most people should be able to keep up. Readership will include frontline workers, professionals of all stripes, and members of the public who have been affected by addiction. But this book was written mainly for other addicts like me. It's all about you—all about us—and why things don't have to be as bad for us as they are. It can all change, but it will come down to you and me, and what we are willing to do. This is not another recovery book—we have plenty of those. While recovery issues are discussed in length, this book is mainly a political treatise. The treatment industry and the recovery culture are all taken on, because they are integral to the realities facing addicts today, and also because rewriting those scripts will be central to rewriting the entire story. It's a story that began long ago, and Chapter 7 provides the historical backdrop.

A reader might note a glaring absence: this book does not say much about why people become addicted. Of course that's an important matter, an understanding of which is central to prevention efforts and, in many cases, important to meaningful recovery. Perhaps in another book, I will address that.

Here, though, my goals are more direct and immediate: like blacks, gays, and others, addicts must find some kind of political center. There was a time few would have thought that homosexuals could, yet they did. The system by which addicts are stigmatized follows a well-known pattern: those who get out of the shitter and abstain long term are recruited to put down the rest. I see people in recovery saying things like "Bitch/asshole hasn't suffered enough—a few more beatings/rapes/infections/arrests might do it." Even when the wording is less harsh, the meaning remains. I see strong parallels with how the formerly poor often despise those who still are poor, or persons from marginalized ethnic groups who succeed and integrate might look down at the ones who still live in the ghetto.

Addicts are not the only oppressed group, but they are the only remaining group deemed to benefit from degradation. Although "hitting bottom" is the term applied to addicts, the line of thinking is not new. In fact, it is very old. There was a time when children were said to benefit and learn from beatings and insults ("spare the rod, spoil the child"), wives too ("a beating will set her straight"), blacks ("the boy needs a good whupping"), gays, the mentally ill, the developmentally challenged. Although these groups are still often targets, *at least the official line has changed.* No other group—ethnic, sexual, or other—is said to require degradation as a means to improvement. Since the Enlightenment, our collective political vision has involved doing away with such attitudes, and we addicts represent something special for this reason: arguably the last hurdle in an arduous quest for social justice that began, perhaps, with a revolution in America and another one in France.

While I wrote this book to enlighten the public, I would really like to educate addicts themselves, to politicize them. Despite harsh words I may have for the system in place, I don't deny a strong ambivalence. In fact, I'm counting on it: we are not the kind of civilization that stays too comfortable with oppression and degradation. In its way, the system really tries to help—even the jail system. I see people looking like crap, drained and barely standing, right when they get busted. Eight months later, someone comes out of jail looking like an athlete. The system does try, and I am counting on that. I also count on the fact that my goals are consistent with the kind of civilization we are trying to create. The "get tough" people usually advocate things like forced treatment, and maybe harsher prison sentences. Sorry, but that's just macho light. Few have the balls to advocate anything like large-scale slaughter which, in another time and another place, might actually work. So I'm calling on our civilization to get real: we don't have the collective pluck to deal with things in a really tough way. My agenda is neither moralistic nor bleeding heart, just practical: might as well treat people right.

This book owes a great deal to my recovery crew—the guys who have my back. They used to scrape me off the floor when I was down, and I'm always ready to do it for them. I call them my "war buddies," because when you're up against something that wants to kill you, you get tight fast. It's not a shallow connection, just high speed. Two men can fight in a war together for a few months, never meet for 20 years, but when they do they're still brothers. I love my recovery crew. We're struggling with a demon that wants to take us out. But it's not kind enough to kill us fast. It wants to bleed us, degrade us, make our loved ones cry, take away our dignity, and then, very slowly, suck us dry. *We don't let the bastard win, do we? And this book wouldn't have happened if not for you, because I'd be dead, locked up, or in the middle of a psycho drug run.*

This book is not about my drug life, or about my recovery, but I'll share one story. A friend of mine once tricked his way out of jail. He pretended to have some kind of aneurism, and then acted like he could barely move or talk. He kept it up for 60 days in the joint, sitting in a wheelchair and moving his head around like some unfortunate creature. He'd call me, but even on the phone he'd talk slowly, words disjointed, and poorly pronounced. When it came time for sentencing, the judge figured he'd "suffered enough." So my buddy walked. Then, driving him home, I found out that he first got the idea for this retard act from watching me spazz out on crack. True story! Funny, but also tragic.

Tragedy can change a man. In my twenties I was a drinker, a jock, and an occasional scrapper. I really thought I was a badass. But I found out: alone and trying to score at 3 a.m., surrounded by hustlers who might want an extra piece of me because of skin … Well, I learned because I had to. I'm rougher around the edges today, yet I've managed to retain my humanity. At times, though, it was hard to tell—almost too close to call. Nietzsche said that when battling a monster, it's important not to become a monster. Yeah, and I've been to hell and back. It's good to be back.

I believe in myself—in my fellow crackheads—and believe that things could really change over the next few decades. This book was written for crackers like me. Hey, drunks, poppers, junkies and other needle freaks too—we're not exclusive.

P.

1

"You need to hit bottom"—a myth that kills

What would you think of a doctor who told a cancer patient that treatment of any kind would be a waste of time because the disease is not yet critical? Any intervention at this point would simply interfere with a process that will, in time, produce lots of pain, degradation, and maybe irreparable physical damage. Oh, sure, early intervention might save you the need to have your arm amputated, but losing an arm might be what it takes to change your attitude and make you receptive to treatment.

No matter how insane this approach would be—should I say evil? —it is precisely how the system has traditionally dealt with addictions. With no other medical condition—not even mental illness or neurosis—is the governing idea that the disease must be allowed to cause a great deal of damage in order to prepare someone for help.

For that matter, with no other medical condition is failure of treatment consistently blamed on the patient (more on this in Chapter 3).

Are addictions really all that different from other diseases on this point? Is it really necessary that someone *hit bottom* in order to improve? No, and this one stupid lie has—by means of treatment practice, social policy, societal attitudes, and even "wars" waged by politicians all over the world against drug users—killed millions and caused many more to suffer needlessly. Like I said already: what we're talking about here is genocide. It is a political issue. Try treating any other disadvantaged group this way—gays, immigrants, the physically handicapped, racial minorities, the mentally ill—and you'd be in big trouble. Yet, daily, those addicted to drugs and alcohol are fed a story about how physical suffering, emotional degradation, possibly even HIV infection, are precisely what they need. No politician—or doctor—would dare to suggest the same to another disadvantaged group.

Perhaps the best way to start will be in the form of a reply to a point surfacing in the minds of a few readers: the bottom, we are told, is personal. The idea is that no two persons are the same, that each can handle different amounts of pain or degradation. While certainly true, and possibly conveying an open-minded attitude, this point simply muddles the issue. Since the bottom is absolutely personal, a paper cut could qualify. Seriously, if people have already decided that whatever precedes recovery must be a bottom, then whatever came before recovery will be called a bottom. In philosophy, this is often called circular reasoning: you must hit bottom prior to recovery; you stepped on dog poop prior to recovery; so stepping on poop was your bottom. That's why the 12 Step world speaks of high bottoms, low bottoms, in between ...

The real issue is this. It starts with a no-brainer: if addiction were painless, few would give it up. From there, the system has long assumed that if someone isn't ready to change, more pain must be the answer.

First, I will point out that this doesn't follow: if some pain is needed, that simply means that pain is a necessary ingredient. It does not prove that pain is the only ingredient, or that higher and higher doses of the same are somebody's best hope. Pain is one ingredient, but there are others. In any case, this idiotic—and murderous—line of thinking has long been defended by a hopelessly circular logic. I will repeat it. Bottoms are personal, and must come before recovery, so whatever comes before recovery has to be a bottom.

To get to the truth, we need to engage with facts rather than such useless "reasoning." As promised, I try to keep this whole treatise clear and simple. So here: three of the best predictors of success in recovery are: (1) social support (family and friends have not written you off); (2) social standing (job, status, and so on); and (3) cognitive functioning. While some issues are debatable, this is not. It's simply a fact known to anyone who has studied the matter. A hardcore drunk, junkie, or crack smoker who does not stop while still enjoying those three markers might need some kind of encouragement. However, if those three markers were to fade away, that person would clearly be closer to a real bottom and yet, statistically, *far less likely to achieve abstinence.* Conversely, an addict in dire straits who receives decent housing (or some kind of decent opportunity, even something like a love connection) will be *more likely to kick.* One step away from a "bottom" is more likely to precede positive change than another step in that direction. Yet, somehow, our culture has come to insist that whatever precedes the point of change must be called a bottom (according to this logic, even winning a lottery and meeting the love of one's dreams might be someone's bottom).

Let's use an example that even more people can relate to. Say we have two tobacco smokers, each with a pack-a-day habit. Demographically—age, gender, culture, income—they aren't too different. The only significant difference is this: one person is happily married and happy at work; the other one just got divorced and is worried about getting fired. I think that most readers can guess that the happier individual is a better candidate for quitting smoking. The other one might quit, but probably not right away. Of course there are exceptions, but the odds are overwhelming: people are much *less likely* to leave their addictions when their lives are in turmoil. The truth really is that simple. More pain, more degradation, will lessen someone's chances of getting better.

Why don't people think so? One reason is that information comes from persons in the treatment system and from persons in recovery. People convey what they see. Now, say we torture and degrade 40 addicts and one ends up recovering. Many in the system, which for practical purposes includes the 12 Step fellowships, assume that the pain and degradation made that one success story possible. The person who recovers may also believe that the suffering is what did it. Sorry, but on this score, people are not always very good at interpreting their own stories and experiences (this is discussed in Chapter 4). Yet in people's minds, that one story confirms the myth. Well, it didn't work for the others, the overwhelming majority. Why not? More important, *those 39 are not in sight and play no role in forming the opinions of whoever interacts with the one success story.*

A recap: if people have been led to believe that bottoms are needed, they will interpret everything coming their way from that point of view. Oh, and if someone got to treatment or to 12 Step groups without too much suffering, no problem: that's a high bottom. I want to make this very clear: *no amount of evidence could ever challenge a mindset governed by this kind of circular logic.* The beliefs have nothing to do with evidence. They are rooted in decades of political, social, and religious brainwashing (this history is discussed in Chapter 7).

Let's look at it from another angle. Anyone in the treatment business or the 12 Step world knows about the stopping and starting that normally takes place before long-term abstinence. Often, the process goes on for years. Someone tries something, it helps for a while, but only for a while. Then the person may try something else. That doesn't work forever, and they slide back into hard using or drinking. Once they get to treatment or a meeting, they might be told that it's good that they finally learned that all those efforts were useless—it has to be all or nothing. Right?

Wrong. What happens in such cases is that all the stopping and starting has reduced overall consumption: someone who once smoked 100 bags a year or drank 400 bottles a year has now been smoking 20 to 80 bags a year, or drinking maybe 50 to 300 bottles a year. After a couple of years of that, or even after six months, someone is a bit healthier. Someone's brain is less saturated than it once was. Such a change, even a small one, will improve cognitive functioning and render someone a better candidate for abstinence. Also, those many days clean have given a person a bit of practice. Anyone who has gotten used to staying sober, for even just three or four days here and there, is a step ahead of someone who can't even imagine two whole days without a drink or a blast. Regardless of what many will tell you, every effort at reduction will increase someone's chances of getting clean for good. Plus, it improves things here and now. So even if it never leads to abstinence, it's a good thing in itself—win-win either way.

Think about this: with most medical conditions, something like a 20 percent improvement is considered a huge accomplishment. With addictions, even an 80 percent reduction in use is considered failure.

Why? It interferes with the bottom that's supposed to get people well. But bottoms don't get you well. First, many people don't survive their so-called bottoms. Second, when someone gets well and attributes it to a bottom, it really means that the person does not understand the process of change. Nothing against that person, but human beings do not have the ability to look inside their own souls and tell you exactly why something changed, improved, or got worse. We speculate, and the explanations we offer are typically functions of what we have been taught. Remember, if everyone around you tells you that a bottom had to do it, and especially if these are people who sincerely want to help, there will always be a way to explain your story accordingly.

Let's take a closer look at methadone maintenance, and use it as a model for other harm-reduction initiatives designed to cut down on the amount of using or curtail the overall damage. Here's what methadone tends to do for people. In some cases, it brings real freedom from all the trouble that goes with drugs and the street life. In other cases, it cuts into the damage:

- Someone who used to shoot up six times a day might be shooting up six or seven times a week.
- Someone who used to smoke an eight-ball of crack a day might be smoking that amount once a week and maybe 40 bucks worth on one or two other days.
- Someone who used to boost every day might be boosting once a week.
- A guy who used to knock his girlfriend out every two months or so will switch to bouts of verbal abuse and maybe giving her a hard shove once or twice a year.
- A girl who used to pull two or three tricks a day is now doing two or three a week.

It isn't pretty, but you get the picture. In many cases, it's all we've got. Methadone has been shown to reduce arrest rates and time spent in jail. Many people refuse to see that and say: Well, so and so is still shooting up, smoking crack, stealing, so what's the difference? Well, even a 5 percent reduction would be something. In many cases, however, the reduction in bad behaviors is over 90 percent. With no other medical condition would such improvements be dismissed. Yet, once more, with addictions, everything short of complete success is treated as failure.

Imagine if someone dependent on a wheelchair worked hard, reclaimed 45 percent of their former abilities, and could now walk—though slowly, with a cane, and only for short distances. Everyone would cheer, and the professionals who helped the person achieve this would be considered to have done well. Who would say: "He's not walking perfectly so what's the point? Might as well break his fucking legs until he learns the real deal and gets it right."

What kind of monster, or idiot, would say such a thing? Yet, when an addict shows a 45 percent improvement, people quickly say the kinds of things that only monsters and idiots would say. I am not suggesting that everyone who says these things is evil or stupid. On the contrary, people have been brainwashed by a nasty, idiotic system. This book is all about how that takes place, and how to put an end to it.

For now, let's get back to the methadone situation. If someone were to badger 20 methadone patients to give it up—because "that's still drug use," "it's not a real solution," etc. —here is what is likely to occur: 1 of those 20 might kick and do very well. A few others won't like the change and quickly get back on the methadone. The rest will resume old patterns, and from there it might not be easy to reconnect with the system. So:

- Someone who was shooting up six or seven times a week will be back to smashing six times a day.
- Someone who was smoking crack sporadically will be back to smoking full time.
- The once-a-week booster will be back to fulltime crime.
- Some woman out there will get six *easily preventable* beatings thanks to someone's preaching.
- The working girl will be back to selling herself fulltime.

Well, at least they got one person to kick and lead a healthy life, right? No—dead wrong! The abstinence pushers would like to take credit for these few success stories. However, statistically, 1 in 20 (give or take) is likely to move in that direction within a reasonable time frame. Nobody does well with abstinence, and then keeps it up, because of someone's badgering. If that person kicked *and got better,* it's because it was that person's time—everyone has their own process. This lucky soul might even believe that the badgering triggered the process, but that proves nothing. The recovery process runs deeply, at levels we still don't fully comprehend. People rarely know why they got better, (something this book also explains in Chapters 3 and 4).

Instead of taking credit for a success story that was already in the cards, certain individuals should in fact take responsibility for what they did cause:

- They should apologize—face to face—to third, fourth, and fifth parties who contracted hepatitis or HIV because of all that extra smashing.
- They should apologize—face to face—to someone who was able to hold down a job or start school despite sporadic crack use and who is now in jail.
- They should apologize—face to face—to the woman who got beat up six times last year because of their preaching.
- They should apologize—face to face—to a girl who had taken a real step in the direction of maybe never selling herself again.

What they shouldn't do is take credit for that one success story. Typically, those who push this tripe will take credit for that one case and never take responsibility for all the misery, arrests, beatings, and murders they cause. Why? Oh, yeah, they are helping people hit bottom. Well, bottoming out is not what gets people ready to change. That's the truth. Forget all the bullshit you've been fed. The recovery process is long. It usually starts well before someone gets clean or goes to treatment or a meeting. Anything one can do to reduce the damage along the way is good for two reasons:

1. Damage is reduced (infections, you name it—that's good, right?).
2. Reducing the damage here and now will increase—*and not decrease*—a person's chances of achieving abstinence sometime down the road.

With no other medical condition does the favored approach involve allowing—or actively encouraging (!)—a disease to do as much harm as possible. There are so many repercussions to this mindset, but I will end this chapter with one example and one thought.

The example: Consider the attention devoted to the effects of substance abuse on unborn children. Now, women (including pregnant women) are far less likely to abuse substances when in a safe and healthy environment. Beyond this, nonbiased studies have been reaching similar conclusions: a pregnant woman who smokes crack, yet has a safe home and receives proper medical attention and good nutrition, is far more likely to produce a healthy child than is a drug-free woman who eats very poorly and has little or no prenatal care. This reality is accentuated if someone must deal with outright homelessness or physical abuse. My point is not that it's OK to abuse substances when you're pregnant. *IT'S NOT OK!* But this kind of thing *happens more often, and the damage gets worse, because society still feels a need to push addicts in the direction of some kind of bottom.* It even affects homeless, pregnant women who don't use drugs, because they are often treated by the system as though they do. No amount of preaching can alter the fact that this whole way of thinking has had devastating effects on addicts, on children, and also on society at large.

The thought: If only pain and degradation will save an addict—if that's what it must take to get that person to take care of his or her children and lead a happy life—then the next time you see a pathetic, smelly drunk stumbling along the street, you should walk over there, kick him in the nuts, and break a few of his fingers. You won't, will you? And you wouldn't support such behavior on the part of professionals. But if bottoming out is the answer, your attitude is simply a cop-out. In fact, your attitude is healthy: not too far below the surface, you understand that this can't be the answer. Your instincts are right. The 20th century was wrong. And by the time you finish this book, you will understand perfectly.

2

Abstinence is the only realistic solution— biggest lie in the business

Check out a few Alcoholics Anonymous (AA), Narcotics Anonymous (NA), or Cocaine Anonymous (NA) meetings. Look around. Or, just ask anyone you know who has participated in these group sessions. For every person there who has two years or more "clean and sober," you will run a across 10 or 20 who slip now and then but keep going back. The slips may occur every six months, or once a week, but what this amounts to is a *serious reduction in use from what went on before*—a reduction that people are far more likely to keep up than nonstop abstinence. Look at the numbers: 20 to 1, 10 to 1 *at least*. Yet a member of one of these fellowships will look a newcomer straight in the eye and say that reduction is impossible, unrealistic, and that long-term abstinence is your only chance. Huh? Most people who say this are sincere, so how are they able to dismiss the evidence right in front of their noses? Well, remember what I said about brainwashing? We are dealing with powerful, culturally induced myths.

You see, everything that a person perceives, sees, hears, and tastes is influenced by what that person has been led to believe. How we interpret details will always be marked by what we have been taught to expect. For this reason, it is very dangerous to trust anybody's experience at face value. Serious verification is necessary, no matter how sincere the person may be. What would you say if I told you that *The Man* uses your own *experience* as a weapon against you? (more on this in Chapter 4)

One thought creeping into a few readers' minds is this: all of the results just mentioned, the many cases of reduction, are generated by telling people to shoot for abstinence; if we let the cat out of the bag, the situation would worsen. Wrong. Treatment programs that allow everyone to set their own goals—moderation, stop-start, abstinence—will end up with just as many cases of long-term (say two years) abstinence as will programs that insist on abstinence only (in either case, 1 in 20—give or take). Where someone starts out in recovery seems to have little bearing on where they end up.

An acknowledgement of these many cases of reduction need not interfere with any individual's abstinence—if they seek it and maintain it, that's great.

One thing that everyone should understand: all of the harm-reduction initiatives—methadone, moderation management, needle exchange, you name it—were not founded on the idea that they necessarily "work" (whatever that might mean—try defining it). Such initiatives have been a response to a proven fact: *abstinence-oriented interventions have failed consistently over the years.* They don't work. Anyone with experience in 12 Step fellowships, or with the treatment industry, has learned this much: if there are 20 newbies in the room, two years from now maybe 1 will still be clean. This means that 95 percent don't make it. Some treatment workers even warn clients on the first day: "Only 1 of 20 of you will make it." Well, if abstinence is the only marker for success, that's absolutely right.

Oh, we're told that all those others *could have, and should have, and would have* ... So it's their fault, right? Wrong (more on this in Chapter 3). Addiction is the only medical condition where failure of treatment is consistently blamed on the patient. On top of this, if one can be helped while 19 must be condemned to degradation, misery, and possible death, then by what warped standard can this be called a success? And we never really know what someone could have done. We only know what they did in fact do. The rest is speculation, and in this case, the speculation is often rooted in wish fulfillment. We are now in the early 21st century, so let's get real: the 12 Step movement has had almost 80 years to get it together, and it still produces the same results. Assorted professional treatment initiatives have been around even longer—same deal. An approach to any medical condition that fails 95 percent of the time is not a successful intervention. It just isn't.

Fortunately, despite all the lies you've been told, the other 19 addicts can indeed be helped—not in 10 years if they bottom out, but right here, right now. An alternative approach, one that acknowledges reality, can still make room for abstinence—and we already know that such approaches generate comparable abstinence results. The only difference is that they do a better job of taking care of everyone else.

Well, it would be hard to do worse. The governing wisdom has long been that if you can't abstain completely, then take a hike, suffer, pick up a virus, run someone over while you're drunk ... and maybe then you'll get the picture. For real, that's essentially what addicts and alcoholics are told. Stop and think: are we in the Dark Ages? Are we still the type of people who whip slaves till they practically die, or burn people at the stake who don't conform? Well, in our dealings with addictions, such attitudes and practices still reverberate (you'll learn why in Chapter 7).

People who are really trying get better are often kicked out of treatment for one or two slips. That's not good policy. That's bullshit. In some places, it's getting worse: many detox centers don't even allow people to step out for a smoke—because that's still considered using.

Since all this nonsense is founded upon an abstinence principle, maybe we should achieve some clarity on what that means. Note that many people who are considered abstinent will still drink coffee or smoke cigarettes. Sugar might be OK, too. Of course, many puritans have picked up on this and have come up with some very stringent definitions of sobriety: no cigarettes, no coffee, etc. (that's a bad idea, and discussed more thoroughly in Chapter 9).

For now, I wish to draw attention to another point—the understanding of which will be central to any decent and sensible approach to addictions in this new century. The late 20th century witnessed a rebirth of age-old wisdom: many behaviors, such as gambling, sex, and even videogames, can take over someone's life and do serious harm. So it makes little sense to single out drug and alcohol use. In 1750, any old priest or granny could have told you that. More recently, it had to be "proven" by experts, recounted by witnesses, and discussed by concerned citizens everywhere. Well, at least we've figured it out. Gambling and sex have perhaps received the most attention. But videogames, the Internet, shopping, eating, exercise—these and many other activities are increasingly being recognized as addictive to many and able to seriously damage people's lives.

With this awareness, a standard—or paradigm—invoked in the 20th century no longer makes sense: to focus exclusively on substance addiction is to miss the point. Ironically, substance addicts themselves, including AA and NA members, have helped to raise awareness in these matters. Most people in those fellowships understand that acting out sexually, gambling compulsively, violence, and a range of other behaviors can be just as unhealthy for them as drug and alcohol use. So we are told: clean time does not equal recovery. Fair enough, there is more to recovery than that. But what do we mean by *clean time* here? Now that other behaviors have been targeted, and rightly so, are we seriously to believe that someone who gambled compulsively for a whole weekend has remained clean, yet someone who smoked one little joint should start counting clean days all over?

I recall when someone I knew celebrated 18 years clean in NA. In Gamblers Anonymous (GA), they would have laughed. You see, my friends and I had to dog him and be there for him when he was gambling hard and hiding from the world—isolating, isolating, isolating. By what standard did this person have "18 years"? Only by a standard that singles out booze and dope. Yet, by now, practically everyone in recovery knows that it's not that simple.

We are left with a very curious situation. Everyone knows that recovery is way more complex than just clean time. Everyone knows that there are many things that an addict can do that would be much worse than a small slip on booze or dope. Yet even the treatment system insists on pure abstinence from psychoactive substances. Oh, they try to curtail other behaviors, but let's get real. Do you know anyone who hasn't "relapsed" somehow—sex, gambling, dope, anger, work, booze, love, overeating, undereating—in the last three years? At this point, it's not even about sickness. It's called being human.

So we are up against an unrealistic standard. If we take seriously the idea that many behaviors are potentially addictive, abstinence becomes a ridiculous goal. It no longer makes sense to single out booze and dope. And there's nothing wrong with people who slip on a substance. Those same people might have gambled less, or had fewer unhealthy sexual relations, than those who didn't get drunk or high. People slipping—on weed, sex, booze, gambling, crack, shopping, overeating, etc. —are not the problem. *The abstinence principle is the problem.*

Think with me: if you really *think it through,* you'll see that "abstinence" makes no sense. The idea may have served a purpose in its day. But we are now in a different world, taking on many different challenges, and abstinence will no longer work as an ideal. We need something better, something real.

If we are to get serious about helping people overcome unhealthy behaviors, then we should be realistic about the goals we set. Since pure abstinence from all maladaptive behavior is unrealistic—and since any such behavior can be just as harmful and addictive as drug or alcohol use—improvement must be the goal. Progress, growth—that's what recovery is about. Not purity. Not perfection. Not just abstinence (this matter is addressed in Chapter 9).

Again, let's all take seriously the idea that many behaviors can be just as dangerous and compulsive as substance abuse, and then ask ourselves: how many people do I know who have been "abstinent" from everything compulsive and harmful for 10 years? I'll go first: people with lobotomies, people in comas, and, oh yeah, dead people. OK, your turn.

This one needs a recap: if about 1 of every 20 addicts and alcoholics manage to abstain for two years, and if the few who do abstain will, here and there, slide into other behaviors that are just as harmful over the course of that time, then is everybody a failure? Do we all suck? Well, like it or not, the current standard for recovery—abstinence—is rigged from the start to make failures of us all.

Addicts themselves should take note: if society has long measured us against a standard that is guaranteed to make us look like losers, we have two options: (1) decide once and for all that we're a bunch of losers who don't stand a chance; or (2) reply to society's expectations with, hmm … something pertaining to fellatio.

It's our affliction. It's our future. And if we decide that we will no longer be society's collective bitch, the one group that everyone still has a right to despise, then maybe it's time to step up. Look at it this way: if we are perceived in such negative terms, it has much to do with our own willingness to pay lip service to the very standards used to keep us down. *Think it over. I haven't missed a thing here.*

Everybody slips one way or another. That's life. That's being human. The abstinence principle is not only unrealistic: it is responsible for much of the pain, suffering, and death that have accompanied the 20th century approach to addiction. Hitting bottom, abstinence—it's all part of one big, ugly picture. And it all must go.

3

Treatment produces abstinence—the second biggest lie

Say you had a habit in 1890. Whether your poison was alcohol, opiates, or cocaine, your chances of kicking weren't much different from what they would be today. It might be a little bit better now, but not by much. All of our combined efforts—treatment, psychiatry, 12 Step fellowships, detoxification units, addiction chatter all over the media—have maybe knocked someone's chances of getting and staying clean up by 3 or 4 percentage points. Is that a hard figure? No, just an estimate. Exact numbers are obviously unattainable. I am though, among other things, a historian of addiction. What I can tell you is that people have been giving up their addictions since the dawn of history, and that community, church, and a range of other engagements have typically been just about as effective in generating long-term abstinence as everything we have in place right now. I have yet to meet another scholar of addiction or its history who has seriously challenged me on this issue (some think your chances were a bit better in the old days). This is not the place to discuss history in length. As promised, sources are provided at the end for anyone wishing to study up and reach their own conclusions.

It is important to think of recovery as a process, one that usually begins well before someone gets clean, or has ever gone to treatment or a self-help group. What our interventions actually do is tweak a process that is, for the most part, independent of external efforts. This point can be brought home by reference to something that everyone in the business seems to know: if a person isn't quite ready to change their lifestyle and behavior, there isn't much we can do beyond adding slightly to their motivation.

Dealing with Addiction

What we still cannot do is generate readiness to change.

Anyone who finds a way to generate "readiness"—I mean a real kick-starter, not just a nudge—would be up for a Nobel Prize. Millions all over the world could be saved immediately. From there, what applied to addiction could probably be adjusted to address mental illness and many other difficulties. So it is very important that you, the reader, understand this: if we were to find a quick and reliable way to generate readiness, the discovery would be as significant as the discovery of germs and all the vaccines that followed. Really, it would be that big.

I've often mused that this reality has something to do with the popularity of the "you have to hit bottom" nonsense. People are frustrated, so they lash out: "I guess she hasn't suffered enough"; "The addiction hasn't kicked the shit out of him enough"; "It's unfortunate, but another rape might be what it'll take to get her thinking straight"; "Tough love is what that punk needs." I've heard this kind of talk and much worse. If you have no experience on the recovery scene yourself, just ask someone who does.

What would you think of someone who spoke this way about the mentally ill, the physically disabled, Hispanics, or gays? There was a time when it was quite acceptable to direct such talk at these groups. It seems that addicts are still an acceptable target. Funny how in crackhead and junkie circles, racist and other types of prejudiced terms are often rampant. From what I've seen, even people to whom the terms might apply usually don't care too much. See, when you put a crack pipe into your mouth, or a needle into your arm, you turn yourself into the biggest nigger there is. You got to feel sorry for someone who can sweat skin after having been a crackhead (some do, of course, but it just leaves me puzzled).

It is in this social context that treatment is said to "work." Hmm … if by that we mean at least two years of abstinence, it might work 5 percent of the time (that's a generous estimate). What about the other 95 percent? They are expendable. With no other affliction, and with no other disadvantaged group, would such a pathetic outcome be deemed a success.

Now, let's have a look at the success, the 5 percent. It is well-known that most cases of recovery—including cases of long-term abstinence—are achieved without professional intervention or self-help group participation. It's hard to pin it down, but our best estimates suggest that for every alcoholic or drug addict who gets clean through treatment, 12 Step groups, or a combination of both, there are *at least* two who get there without such help. And, yes, many of the very hardest cases get better by means of what has been labeled "natural recovery." It seems that addictions follow a trajectory that we don't fully understand: in a nutshell, addictions often start innocently, progress to destructive levels, and then very often taper off. So someone who used to be drunk every day might later be drunk only once a week. After a while, even that might go. This might be hard for many readers to accept, but *most of the 5 percent who got clean with treatment or 12 Step groups would have gotten there anyway.* Think about it: even the treatment industry will admit that they can't do anything for someone who isn't ready. *Follow that thought*: the 1 in 20 who are ready are probably on track for sobering up. One way or another, it would likely happen. That's what *readiness* is all about. All treatment can do is tweak a process that runs more deeply than any of our best knowledge. For real: it's something that we can manipulate slightly, but never control. We seem to be able to improve the odds, but only by a small margin. Maybe someday that will change, but it hasn't yet.

Now, many in recovery insist that they know what worked for them. They will tell you that they owe their current sobriety or clean time to a treatment institution or a 12 Step group. "I don't know much, but I know what worked for me." It sounds good. It's catchy. But that doesn't make it true. You see, people don't really know what worked for them. If you had the ability to look inside your soul, identify what caused what, which in turn led to a new attitude and healthy behavior, you would be more than human. You would be some kind of superior being. A team of experts—biologists, psychiatrists, spiritualists, sociologists—could study one person fulltime for 10 years, and even then any account of why things happened the way they did would be opinion. There is no way to establish certainty.

People are normally unaware of such things and jump to conclusions. That is understandable. What is less acceptable (to me) is a system that allows people these delusions, and in fact fosters these delusions, in ways that do real harm to those people (this is explained more thoroughly in Chapter 4).

Here, a little medical history will have to do. For the longest time, humanity had so-called remedies for diseases like the flu, chicken pox, and measles. The remedies didn't do much, and in the West at least, medicine failed even to distinguish between different diseases. All medicine could offer were haphazard practices, usually mixed up with Christian stuff in the West, shaman stuff somewhere else, and so on. But people typically would do what they were told and usually they got better. So you'd thank your doctor for curing you of the flu, or your child of the measles. It took centuries for humanity to finally understand that many diseases run a course: they start small, peak out, and then recede. In years gone by, you may have spent the rest of your life worshiping the doctor and recommending him to others, even though your flu receded for reasons that had nothing to do with what the doctor did. In fairness to the doctor, he didn't know either. He gave people his best, and saw decent results all his life.

Recap: it took a long time for humanity to identify specific diseases and their trajectories. Until we understood this, for thousands of years there was nothing obvious about any of it. When people got better, they were certain that their doctors or religious figures were the cause. No conspiracy needed, because the authority figures had reason to believe it as well.

From here, let's turn to a little history of mental disease. For the longest time, talk therapists and other professionals were taking credit for curing depression and other such things. Only later did we learn, for example, that some types of depression are cyclical. Some even run on a five-year schedule (!). Horribly depressed people would slowly get better and give some shrink credit for the change.

You see, when people are ready to change, typically they get busy. Subsequently, they will attribute the changes to the activities in which they engaged. That, however, is a huge assumption. Maybe sometimes it's your activity that caused a change, but at other times you are riding a process that is largely indifferent to your behaviors. The flu recedes in due course, the depression lifts after a few years—in either case, the disease might not give a rat's ass whether you did push-ups or meditated. It's just doing its thing, and too bad if you desperately want to believe that you were in control.

A good example might be AA's cofounder, Bill Wilson. He had a powerful spiritual experience and, *possibly,* that's what helped to keep him off the booze. But his recurring bouts of depression—often leaving him emotionally paralyzed to the point where his wife had to struggle just to get him out of bed—came and went as such diseases often do. Like arthritis, depression can wax and wane—with either disease, our activities make a difference but will not carry the day completely.

More recently still, we have learned that addictions often have such trajectories. They get stronger and then recede. Sometimes it's a lifelong process of progression and then remission. At other times it's intermittent—back and forth for years and years. It's a good bet that in many cases—though not every case—the difference between long-term abstinence and intermittent relapse has far more to do with biology than the 20th century was willing to admit. We no longer blame people for sliding back into depressive states. We used to and were wrong to do so. Now, instead, *we work within the depressive relapse to make it as painless as possible.* That's the right approach. We must turn in that direction with addictions as well.

Again, people have long known that addictions are typically progressive: they get worse over time. What we have learned since is that they are also regressive: after a while, they typically recede. So the alcoholic either stops completely or drinks a lot less. Many will tell you that drinking less often will only work for a while, and in many cases that's true. However, the same can be said about stopping completely—how many AA or NA members do you know with over 20 years of abstinence? It happens, but it's rare. What we really seem to be learning is that, like many illnesses, addictions wax and wane. They get better, and then get worse. They might leave for a few months or several years, and then they might come back.

It is, for this reason, very hard to tell in any one case whether treatment or 12 Step groups had anything to do with an improvement. In any one case, they might have. But, given everything we've learned, it is fair to say that in a majority of cases in which people get better after engaging with any so-called program of recovery ... well, they got busy because they were changing. *They didn't change because they got busy.* The activity might help a little, but it does not cause the change. This change is, in fact, caused by a process that runs more deeply than our own activities. That's why people were getting clean and sober almost as frequently in the 18th and 19th centuries as they are today.

Many in the treatment industry, and even in the 12 Step world, will tell you that they have a "program" that works for anyone who follows it *to the letter*. First, since the program includes abstinence, obviously anyone who has abstained has, you know, abstained. So what? Remember what I told you about circular reasoning? But there is more. For years and years, therapists were taking credit for alleviating cases of depression that were largely unaffected by therapy. That's understandable, and I don't mean to rip those therapists. They really had no way of knowing. I simply want you to consider the logic: when someone's depression lifted, it was attributed to adherence to a program—*doing the do things*. When someone got worse, well, it was said to be due to having stopped doing those things. No! If anything, they stopped doing stuff because the illness was coming back. For a long time though, depression patients often took the blame for the recurrence of feelings and behaviors that had little to do with their adherence to any program of recovery. In mental illness, we've done a decent job of getting past that error. In addictions we have not.

There is a formula for such delusions that everyone should understand. Recall again what I told you about circular reasoning. Now, some statements are simply not *falsifiable*. This means that a belief system is set up in such a way that no one could ever poke a hole in it. If "X" happens, that proves the statement to be true. If the opposite of X happens, that also proves the statement to be true. Here's how it can work in the addiction field. When a practitioner says the program always works, but some people don't work the program, the statement is not falsifiable. Follow me: say the program comprises 20 "do things." Say someone is doing 17 of them. If that person does well, that is said to be because of those 17 items. This, in turn, is said to "prove" that the program worked. Now, if that same person were to slip and slide, the absence of 3 remaining items would be blamed. *This is said to prove that not doing those 3 things caused a relapse.* Regardless of whether the result is X or NOT X, the result can be used to prove that the program itself never fails. Even if someone does only 4 of 20 and is successful, those 4 things can be said to cause abstinence. If someone else is doing 19 of 20 and starts to relapse, the one remaining item can be identified as having caused the relapse. There is no such thing as perfect adherence to any program, so there is always a way out for those who would defend the program. Even if someone is doing 20 of 20 items, there is no way each item is being done perfectly. So there is always an absence— "resistance" in psychoanalysis, "reservation" in 12 Step, "negativity" in other circles—upon which a relapse can be blamed. Here's what you get: a system that can withstand any evidence that comes. If treatment practitioners are able to convince everyone that the program (which might be cognitive behavioral, 12 Step, psychoanalytical, or something else) never fails, people will interpret everything that comes their way accordingly.

"I know what worked for me." No, you don't. But maybe the system wants you to think that you know. How's that for a play? (the very next chapter will explain this more clearly).

For now, I will simply note that former Chinese leader Deng Xiaoping lived to 93 and would have been happy to tell you that chain smoking worked for him. A firm believer in the benefits of smoking, Deng was proud of his habit and recommended it to others.

Is addiction treatment useless? Far from it. It does increase (however slightly) someone's chances of achieving long-term abstinence. Most important is an effect that is rarely recognized: even if only 1 in 20 stays clean, most of the others have reduced their use. Whether that reduction is 5 percent or a whopping 90 percent, a great deal has been accomplished. Although we still have no way of pushing up the long-term abstinence totals, we can do wonders mitigating the damage along the way. With any other medical condition, if treatment leads to a 50 percent improvement, it's called successful. With addiction, even a 95 percent reduction in crack or alcohol use is deemed a failure. So when someone who used to get tipsy or high every day is now doing it every 20 days, it's considered a failure. Why? This is the kind of result that treatment—and even 12 Step meeting attendance—can accomplish in many cases. It's a realistic goal. As for abstinence, that seems to happen when the disease is ready to recede for real. In order to generate long-term abstinence, someone would have to generate readiness. Nobody knows how, as every professional and every AA member can attest: if you're not ready, there isn't much anyone can do about it.

But treatment can help. Take depression. If it's deep-seated, probably with a strong biological component, only in rare cases will you be able to simply talk someone out of being depressed. However, the intensity of it all can be mitigated with talk therapy, medication, or both. Or, how about this: you see a guy in a park swatting at imaginary objects in the air—try talking him out of it, tell him it's in his head. That won't work, but there are ways to make these episodes less unpleasant and even less frequent. With addictions, it's a lot like that: when someone is active—not ready to kick—the odds are very slim that you will get that person to kick. We are dealing with subcognitive processes that are still not well understood. The intensity and frequency of using can, however, be mitigated. That's called harm reduction. The worst—nastiest, stupidest—thing you can do is tell an addict in that state to use hard and heavy, damage and degrade herself, in order to achieve a bottom. That's not an achievement. And to repeat: people will not be more likely to end up abstaining long term because of this—every bit of real knowledge we have suggests that these bottoms reduce people's odds of getting there.

So isn't it about time to get real? We can't simply conjure up abstinence, because we can't create readiness. That will be a major challenge for this century, and if we find a way, it'll be a huge accomplishment. In the meantime, what we can do is mitigate the damage until readiness kicks in: fewer infections, fewer arrests, fewer beatings, fewer deaths, fewer rapes; more employment, more going to school, more families reunited. I call that a result.

Remember again what everyone already knows: if someone isn't ready to change, no approach is likely to work. The flip side of this reality has been surfacing in more recent studies: if someone is ready, it probably won't matter whether the person engages in cognitive behavioral therapy, 12 Step, or something else. Studies have been confirming this. Plus, the fact that at least two of three addicts and alcoholics who achieve abstinence do it without treatment or self-help groups also adds weight to the idea that the choice of activity is far less important than the state of readiness.

If people get clean without professional help, it has a lot to do with the social support they receive from family and friends. Such support does seem to help, both with abstinence and reduction. This is why group therapy and 12 Step fellowships are so popular: connecting with other people is considerably more important than any so-called program of recovery. Even in the 12 Step world, for example, people are told that they must pass on the program to others—give it away.

Whether they know it or not, it's that *social connection* that is most helpful to their recovery.

Now some may object, saying that certain treatment organizations claim to produce very high abstinence rates. In fact, there is little difference on this score between the many places out there (except cost—you can purchase comfort, but not a better cure rate).

First, you need to understand how the numbers can be crunched. I will try to keep it simple. There is the issue of "intention to treat." Essentially, if 40 people show up for assessment and only 30 end up in treatment, do those lost souls count as failures? If not, then what about those who drop out of the program (or get kicked out) one quarter of the way through, or halfway through? A stated success rate can be improved simply by pushing the bar in one direction. But here's my favorite: someone tells you that they keep track of former clients. After five years, 25 percent of them are still clean and another 40 percent slipped a few times but are doing well. Thirty-five percent of them are actively drinking or using and not doing well at all. This seems like an amazing success rate. Well, I ask (they hate it when I do this): what percentage of your clientele are you in touch with after five years? Silence. *Come on.* "Well, maybe 15 percent. All I can tell you is what we know." Hmmm ... does it not occur to this person that the 85 percent who can't be found are maybe not doing as well as the 15 percent who've kept in touch? It's nice that a big chunk of that minority is doing well, but it proves nothing.

I won't discuss every little trick used to generate groovy numbers. I'll simply draw your attention to one fact: any treatment operation that generated abnormally high abstinence rates, and proved something by keeping it up for years, will have solved the "readiness riddle." That's the only way it could be done: they would have found a way to generate—create—readiness to change. The people involved would be up for Nobel Prizes, tons of cash, and maybe movie contracts. And, no, the "system" isn't keeping such knowledge down or ignoring it. Such results—if they were real—would attract scientists from all over (myself included), media, and all kinds of entrepreneurs out to make a killing. Official medical bodies (e.g., psychiatric) would want to know, simply because better results are good PR and a great way to justify funding. Everyone would win. Well, everyone except people who make stuff up.

It is important to recall a point already made: moderation management and all of those other initiatives that don't require pure abstinence have simply been responses to the fact that in a vast majority of cases, abstinence won't happen. Instead of blaming 19 of 20 clients for the next hundred years, the system should opt to engage with reality rather than with fantasies about supposedly infallible programs.

Another—very important—matter: often the best solution is a substitute drug. This can be methadone, an antidepressant, marijuana, a tranquilizer, or something else. Yet, currently, such approaches are viewed suspiciously or rejected outright by many in the field simply because they are inconsistent with an abstinence principle—one more reason to leave that principle behind (more on this in Chapters 8 and 9).

One more point before ending this chapter. There is a well-known phenomenon in addiction treatment: the *abstinence violation effect.* Those who cling tenaciously to abstinence are likely to do worse when they slip than those who are more relaxed about it. Talk to anyone in the 12 Step movement, and they can tell you that much: people with rigid belief systems might stay clean a bit longer, but when they fall, they fall harder and for longer.

It gets worse when people's heads are filled with propaganda about how, if they ever use, any attempt to control it will be a wasted effort. *"Might as well hit a hard bottom. Suck your bank account, and your body, dry. Don't kid yourself, there's no such thing as controlled use for an addict."*

Now, there is some truth to that, which is why it's called addiction. But how true this is, how rough it has to be, will be affected by what one has been taught to believe. You see, efforts to control and cut back can, in fact, do wonders, but they are far more likely to be futile if an addict has been led to believe that they must be futile. Now, say an addict or alcoholic goes to a treatment center at a young age and then does well for a while. Grateful for the help, this innocent soul will be inclined to believe that control and reduction are impossible—mainly because the treatment people who have earned his trust and respect have said so. After a relapse, the young follow thinks: "Why bother? I'll get clean after I've drained myself and hit another bottom." After a few years of degradation, he sobers up. Now he's even more certain that the treatment people were right, since it played out just like they said it would. Next time, the prediction becomes even more "true." I know people in their forties and fifties who have struggled with addictions all their lives, doing well for a few years and then sliding for a few. It's hard to tell, in any one case, how much extra damage was done by the propaganda. But the power of therapeutic suggestion should never be underestimated. Believing that you can't win a football game will increase your chances of losing, and the same process applies right here. Some damage would obviously happen no matter what. Just as obviously, some of the damage was caused by suggestion—maybe only 5 percent, maybe as much as 90 percent. It is hard to say in any one case.

But here and there, the picture has been clear to me. I see people grateful to treatment centers from 10 or even 25 years back. They believe most of what they had been told there. Their slips are hard and nasty, typically lasting at least one or two years. But then I explain that maybe it doesn't have to be that bad. Maybe the relapses are only that bad because of the mind-fuck. Guess what? Sometimes, the next slip isn't so bad—it only lasts a week, or maybe two months, plus the using isn't as hardcore. It's sad that the information came late, because businesses have gone under, health has been compromised, and family alienated. In such cases, my professional opinion is that while certain treatment centers *might have had* something to do with why these people first got clean, the same centers had much more to do with making their lives far more tragic than necessary.

Dr. Pete says: "They're not the ones who fixed you up—they're the ones who fucked you up!"

Time to wake up.
Time to get busy.

4

"All I have to share is my own experience"—your experience might not mean what you think it does

Knowledge coming from personal experience is valuable. In the addictions field, professional experience is also key. In either case, however, there are strict limits to experiential knowledge. In order to understand the reality of addiction—right here, right now in the early 21st century—one must understand these limits.

The last section already explained why people in recovery are often mistaken when claiming to know why they got better. Sorry if that offends (no, I guess I'm not).

There is another error common to the addiction field. It has been called the *practitioner's fallacy*. Essentially, this fallacy involves mistaking what one sees in a treatment center, or anywhere on the frontlines, for the big picture.

Here's how it can happen. Let's say 100 crackheads visit the same treatment worker. Say the worker tells all of them not to do A, and (hee hee) they all go out and do A. Hey with crackerjacks like me, you know ...

Anyway, let's say that 80 of them get clean and stay happy, and that 20 screw up on dope and really make a mess of their lives. Of course, these are not real numbers. You will get my meaning in a second. Who is likely to go back to the practitioner? Well, the ones who need help. But even more important: the ones who don't need help also believe the practitioner to have been mistaken. The practitioner has probably lost their confidence, maybe even their respect, so even for some kind of follow-up consultation, they are unlikely to go back to that same place. Here's what can happen: 4 of the 80 return for some reason and 12 of the 20 return, for a total of 16. Based on this evidence, the practitioner now believes that 12 of 16 crack smokers who did A screwed up badly. Keep giving the same advice for 10 years—don't do A—and you will get similar feedback for 10 years. A practitioner's long-term experience might be that a vast majority of druggies who do A fail in their recovery, even though the reality is that 80 percent who do A fare quite well.

A few things must be understood. For research purposes, "treatment samples" (samples drawn from people in treatment) are already unreliable because anything from age, race, gender, you name it, can affect who goes in the first place. Also, and more important, as I just explained: a practitioner's professional experience will be biased in favor of reinforcing the practitioner's point of view. Quite simply, the more consistent one's experiences are with what one is told, the more respect for (and faith in) someone will have in that practitioner. From there, people recommend a practitioner—pro or con—to their friends. Once more, everything from race, accent, taste in music—it can all affect whom the practitioner ends up seeing.

This kind of oversight helps to explain why many doctors dealing with addiction and alcoholism a hundred years ago sincerely believed that such people were practically hopeless. They were no more hopeless in 1910 than they are today. Doctors would see those who kept messing up and not those who got better. Among those who got better for a long time, the doctor would maybe see them only years later, right after a relapse. Relying on one's own experience may seem reasonable, but it invariably leads to a skewed picture. This fact was not as well understood a hundred years ago. So we can, for example, forgive someone like the venerable W. D. Silkworth for making inaccurate claims in the AA Big Book. He simply didn't know. But there's no excuse today for practitioners making he same type of error.

OK, but by talking to several frontline people, we'll get a better picture, right? Maybe, but not always. You see, if 200 frontline people have all been trained in the same way, and if they all say "Don't do A," then they will mostly generate the same kind of feedback at work. So, if you go to a convention with 200 practitioners and almost all of them agree that 75 percent of addicts who do X fail and that 90 percent who do Y succeed—well, sorry, but that just doesn't prove anything. Also, what you really need to understand is this: sometimes it's nobody's fault. Much of the situation surrounding addictions today has a lot to do with the *ways in which knowledge and opinions travel innocently from one person to the next.*

Get your head around this: you can have a political strategy, one that works, without any conspiracy behind it. In many ways, that's what we're up against. Think of the picture as involving minute strategies—little puny ones—that may coalesce and form larger ones. Often, certain players have a sense of what helps their agenda and so generate the kind of information (or misinformation) likely to serve that agenda. In principle though, misinformation can feed misinformation without anyone having planned it.

I can't give you a decent account of the ways in which experiential knowledge operates and how it is limited. Sorry for sounding arrogant, but I'm trying to cover a lot of ground here, and I want this book to be short and fun to read—not a drag. Phenomenology and ethnography are two ways to approach this matter. If you're interested, read up and do the work.

What I can do is give you a decent introduction. First, the situation: many people seem to think that the "system" is full of intellectuals and scientists who lack experience with addiction and are hence out of touch. There's some truth to that, but it's a minor issue. The big problem right now is the opposite: the kind of serious knowledge we need is constantly sidelined because the system is packed full of uneducated, or semi-educated, loudmouths who overestimate the importance of their own stories. So people think they know what made them recover, and they don't want to hear any talk about how that kind of insight is humanly impossible. In any single case, you can never know why—that's the truth, but many people don't want to hear it.

But the story is more involved. How many crack users do you think use only on occasion? Maybe you think very few. Maybe you think 1 percent to 10 percent. Wrong. We don't know, but at least 50 percent (and probably much more) use the drug infrequently (and keep that up for years without getting hooked). Talk to any crackhead on the street, and they'll probably say no way. They'll normally tell you that occasional crack users are rare. You see, an occasional user might smoke twice a year, and on each occasion make two trips to a dealer. A hardcore addict might use five days out of seven (and sleep for two days) and on each using day make six trips to a dealer. The occasional user has made four trips a year, while the real crackhead makes 30 trips a week. For occasional users to make an equal impression on hustlers and working girls, they would have to outnumber addicts by a very large margin. Also, people on the street may assume that all occasional crack users end up addicted, but again, that's because those are the ones who eventually show up often enough to make a lasting impression.

So, how does one find out? Ethnographic work has to be done on what are called "hard-to-reach populations"—for example, people who smoke crack or shoot up once in a while but don't brag about it on TV. See what I mean? I've done some ethnography myself, and there are ways to get a sense of a situation. Other researchers do other studies, and often we look for consistency. If five different studies—done by different teams in different cities—show similar results, then we get more confident about our estimates. More work has to be done, but it's a start.

Eventually, the available information may fall into the hands of a serious number cruncher, someone who understands probability theory (among other things). Now, here's the point. This person may not have experience with the addict world, but the information was compiled either by persons who do (like me), or persons who have been trained in ways to connect with populations that might be a little shy at first (it can be done). The number cruncher may be honest enough to say that estimates have to be rough.

Now, who are you gonna believe? A fancy-pants intellectual who hasn't been there, or a *hardcore guy who knows the score, did it the hard way, so don't fuck with me bitch cause I've been around ...*

Well, knowing "the score" from each side, I'll trust the geek. Maybe he's never been anywhere interesting in his life and maybe he's never even smoked a joint. And OK, tough guy, maybe you know a 14-year-old crack ho who could whoop him in a scrap. Too bad: his take on this question will be more reliable than that of a gangster player hardcore mother fucker who's been there and knows what time it is.

For real. What I'm trying to convey here is not a 50/50 figure, and I don't care right now what the exact number might be.

What's the issue? It's a big one. The entire recovery culture has long favored experiential knowledge at the expense of hard, scientific knowledge. My point is not that personal experience has no place, but that we've overdone it. Even among professional treatment workers in the field, few understand the many ways in which firsthand, experiential accounts are limited. In order to make decent use of such accounts, these limits must be understood.

Trouble is, people get upset when told about this. Everyone wants their own experiences to be important. That's just being human. This tendency, however, is accentuated among anyone who has suffered: see, we all want our pain to have meaning. It does have meaning, but not always in the ways we would like it to. Sometimes, our personal accounts are irrelevant, but we want to make a big deal out of them. *Sometimes it's worse: our own stories can be used to keep us down.*

Now, back to the crackhead figures. You're a hardcore player. Yeah, you're all that. And people want to know your thoughts on what percentage of crack users are casual. You say 1 percent, and too bad for that egghead punk who says 50/50. People believe you, take you seriously, and that makes you feel good. But that crazy figure you offer will simply serve to demonize the addict population. Now, a 50 percent addiction rate is still very high—it's not a ploy to belittle the dangers of crack. But a 99 percent rate will make it all look so crazy, and so scary, that harsh laws, police brutality, and all kinds of punitive measures are easier to justify. *All the talk about why addicts have to get degraded and tortured before they're ready to change starts to sound more real.* This way, you just participated in your own degradation, your own demonization. You might feel like somebody is hearing you, validating your point of view. Wake up and smell the coffee: you're not being validated, you're being played.

In the same way, people thinking that they know what worked for them is simply going to buttress an approach to the issue that does little more than justify the degradation of other addicts—addicts just like them.

So, where does this all lead? A sound bite will do. "You need to bottom out. You need to be beaten and broken, raped and shit on, spit on, and fucked up the ass with a broom handle. It'll do you good. We're the kind of people who benefit from torture and degradation." Blacks don't say that to blacks, and Jews don't say that to Jews. But a crackhead will say that to a crackhead, and a junkie will say that to a junkie. And they mean it! These dumbfucks really perceive themselves as wise, enlightened, and, here's my favorite: spiritual. They don't think they've been manipulated by a system that often treats them with about as much respect as Hitler had for Jews. Oh yeah, they have "experience." How did we get here? How could such an absurd situation evolve? (you will understand perfectly after reading Chapter 7).

A reporter who hates gays or Puerto Ricans won't admit it in public. But it's OK to hate us, right? If you want to step up and make a difference, you must never lose sight of that.

The geek who knows the real numbers and another egghead who knows more about recovery than most recovering addicts ever will—they are not the "system" keeping you down. They have the kind of knowledge that could lift us all up, and that's why many in authority will do what they can to sideline them. "Hey, I'm on your side. I'm with the little guy. I'm no fancy talking intellectual. I'm the one who wants your point of view to be heard." It all sounds good, and many people who talk that way are straight up. Many are not. You must learn to distinguish, and this book is all about teaching you how.

You see, in North America we have a strong democratic tradition. Often, the very people who want to jack the poor will make use of populist sentiments and get the poor to vote against themselves. If they make it hard for someone to get an education, and then tell that person that their uneducated point of view is great, the poor sap might buy it. So who needs an education? Not you, not your people, not your kids. *That's the play*—and it can be used on the poor, on blacks, on natives, on crackheads, and on marginal groups that haven't been invented yet. It's a subtle game: using your own experience as a weapon against you!

I end this chapter with a little bit of intellectual and political history. There has long been a tradition in the West of vindicating the perspective of those who have suffered. In itself, that's great. Giving them the last word usually isn't. Now, please think with me. My dad was a Hungarian immigrant who had suffered horribly because of communism. He was an open-minded guy, smart and easy to exchange ideas with. But when it came to communism, he'd often turn into a complete moron. Three years of starving and freezing in a Soviet prison camp probably had something to do with it. Sometimes he'd discuss the matter with detachment, but not too often. He couldn't keep it up long enough to generate real clarity. You could never trust my dad to tell you what the Soviets were about. He hated them too much. He'd smell communism under every rock and every cupboard. I don't mean to stick up for the Soviets. I hated them too (still do, wherever they are). But when I studied Soviet political reality in university, I could leave my feelings at the door and achieve clarity. It would have been unfair to expect my dad to do the same.

Among many Westerners, there has long been a tendency (sometimes well intentioned) to give the afflicted the last word. Unfortunately, anyone who has been burned, beaten, broken, spit on, and shit on by A, might not be the one who can tell you what A is about. We should take that person's perspective into account, give it some due respect, but that's all. What would you make of a criminal trial in which the judge, jury, and prosecutor all had a personal beef with the defendant? What are we to make of recovering addicts who think that they can tell us the score, if "the score" is something that degraded them and their loved ones for decades?

It's OK to respect your own experiences, but you must be clear on when they might be muddled. Otherwise, you will always be manipulated and kept down. You will always be somebody's bitch.

Time to step up.
Make 'em go tizzy.

5

Codependency—a stupid word that doesn't mean anything

Check out a recovery session, professional, 12 Step, or other. You might hear a lot of this: *I, me, work on myself, love myself, speak from the I, all I have to share is my experience, validate myself, help myself before I can help others, I can't love you because I must first learn to love myself.* Apparently, the process is geared to helping people become less self-centered. A while back, when speaking to North Americans, the Dalai Lama suggested that it's best to avoid the word "I" and other such self-referential markers when communicating. I don't agree with him completely, but I am certain that the West right now could use a strong dose of what he has to offer.

Let's start by reminding ourselves that we are social beings. Like dogs and wolves, and unlike cats, we run in packs. Every human being ever born was a member of a group, family, or tribe before any awareness of personal identity. The sense of belonging will always precede the sense of self. Aware only of its desires, a baby or a toddler will have affection—and love—for its caregivers well before it even understands that it, too, is a person just like the big creatures it loves.

So you have to love others before you can love yourself, and too bad for the "me" culture. If you've been through a lot, maybe you need to stop hating yourself, but that's not the same thing. Even in these cases, the best way to get there is to start caring for others. Love won't come to you just because you masturbate a lot. The best way to achieve self-love is to do loving things: take action, and self-love will be the payoff. Again, it's all about the people around you.

Some might not agree. Many in recovery who have been clean and sober for 5 years, 10 years, 15 years, or more—some of whom are 40, 50, or even 65 years old—still sit alone at home each night because they are "not ready" to partner up. What in God's name are we doing to people?

In the 1980s, when all of this codependency business began, over 90 percent of North Americans were said to be codependent. Those who pushed this tripe had a good thing going: admitting it proved that you are codependent, and denying it also proved that you are codependent. I confess to having some grudging respect for that little play.

What really went on was a disgusting attempt to pathologize relationships that were perfectly normal, and to get rich doing it.

The codependency movement could have taken shape nowhere but in the modern West. What we have is probably the most individualistic culture that humanity has ever produced. Free enterprise, "doing it for yourself," "I did it my way"—these platitudes are specific to a certain place and time. Don't get me wrong: I love Western individualism. The freedom of choice, freedom of expression (political, religious, sexual, or other)—these are great achievements. We should, however, be aware that this way of thinking is unusual and does not make for a good standard against which to define pathological conditions. To this day, in many parts of the world, marriages are still arranged and professions handed down through family. In such settings—the kind you would run across throughout most of human history—an attempt to choose one's profession, or one's spouse, is often considered pathological.

The issue here is not which culture we might think is right, who we like, or who we wish to side with. It's about getting a sense of what's natural and what isn't. For example, Western questionnaires often fail to identify alcoholism in other settings simply because our thoughts and terms don't translate: asking someone about losing control over their drinking produces strange results in societies where people are not expected to control their drinking. Controlling your drinking is the job of all your relatives and some of your friends. It's not that people stick their noses into your business, but that everything you do has never even been considered to be your business. Your business is everybody's business. And everybody else's business is your business. If we were to take all that codependency chatter seriously, we'd have to conclude that well over 90 percent of cultures throughout human history have been very sick. In fact, the modern West would be the only place where health could ever be achieved, and even here less than 10 percent are said to qualify. Maybe the codependency pushers should mind their business.

Multicultural centers across the continent—New York, Toronto, Sacramento—are packed full of immigrants for whom some type of "codependency" is a way of life, and certainly not a disease. Maybe someday their children will be more Western, insist on this and that kind of liberty in their teens, and drive these poor immigrants nuts (I think I did something like that to my immigrant parents).

The word "codependent" is used in many ways. Supporting a substance-abusing partner in their addiction is perhaps the original meaning, but the term has come also to target all kinds of relationships—sexual, friendship, professional. A problem with the entire notion of codependency is that it makes sense only in contrast to a conception of personal autonomy that is, first, unrealistic (that's why pretty well everyone is codependent), and, second, specific to the modern West. Here, a certain type of independence is often considered essential to emotional health and wellbeing—pesky relatives are not.

Yet the presence of pesky relatives, who are now often derided as codependent, is a good predictor of success in the achievement of one's recovery goals. No matter what you've been told, if two addicts or alcoholics in recovery are pretty well identical according to other measures of likely success, the one with more pesky, interloping relatives will be more likely to do well.

A look at the meaning of "motivation" might help you to understand why. For the achievement of treatment goals, one's initial motivation is not a very good predictor of long-term success. In fairness, motivation is hard to measure (Are you motivated to get better? —*Hmmm ... yes! Did I get that one right?*). Still, there are ways to distinguish between those who are motivated and those who are apathetic. More important is this: motivation tends to be fleeting. It comes and goes, ebbs and flows. There is no way to tell whether someone's motivational state will change. Social support—which includes familial support—is an excellent predictor of long-term, reliable motivation. Motivation may in some ways come from within, but it also comes into us from the outside. *It's all about other people, and not just: me, me, me ...*

Perhaps the most hurtful message associated with this movement is one that had already been around before codependency was invented. The message has simply gotten louder over the last few decades: if you want to recover, you must do it for yourself and not for anyone else. Well, half the people I know in recovery would not be clean if they didn't have kids. Nothing wrong with that. Ask anyone who's done hard time whether they'd bother to stay clean during a long stint in solitary if there were any drugs in the cell. Of course they wouldn't. For that matter, even the lowest bitch on the totem pole will take degradation and beatings over long-term isolation. As social beings, we can't be alone. It makes us crazy. It kills us. People growing up in the West, watching cowboy flicks wherein tough guys say things like "A man's gotta do it for himself" might want to recall that for the first five years of his life, the Duke was helpless and totally dependent on his mom. The individualistic one-liners—self-starter, do-it-for-yourself—may ring to true to your ears, but that doesn't mean they are true. It might just mean that your ears have been bent out of shape by the media.

Where does this get us? Here's what one addict might say to another. "If you're not ready to do it our way, then you need to suffer, maybe get shot, busted, infected. Why should I care about you anyway? Fuck you! I'm here for myself." In "Recovery School" addicts are taught to think this way, talk this way, act this way—above all, they are taught to treat each other this way.

Here's something the segregation advocates always knew: to keep the black folks down, you had to split them up. Then, consider how the addicts who get out of the shithole are trained to despise the majority who do not. But when you slip and slide, my friend—and statistically you probably will—where does it all leave you? And there need be no shame in it: everyone falls now and then, one way or another—not just addicts. It's endemic to the human condition. But here's where we do have choice, real choice: must a trip or a slip be compounded by more of the same, must it entail extremes of degradation, or will you stand tall, face it, and roll with it? So I'll leave you with two questions: How do you want to be treated? What do you want to be?

6

"Don't enable the addict"—why not? It's really the only solution

Not too long ago, "enabling" was normally considered a nice gesture, a kind gesture, a good thing to do. You might enable poor kids to go to college, or enable the hungry to eat, grow their own food, and this in turn might enable them to gain more respect for themselves and the people around them. Today, somehow, enabling has come to mean being a sucker, or a control freak. In a *me* culture, that attitude might fit. Yet, as the story goes, the one person in the whole world you must never "enable" is the addict. You'll find out why in the next chapter.

It's high time we all started to enable each other. This might apply to all of humanity, but my goals are more focused. If the rest of the world won't enable my people—my crackheads, my needle freaks—fuck 'em. We can enable ourselves. And, no, this doesn't mean that you help your friend destroy himself, though it might mean you get a lot less preachy. If someone's jonesing, should you shoot her 20 bucks? Up to you—can you spare it? I doubt you'll harm anyone with a move like that, but it's up to you in each case. That is a minor issue anyway, and this chapter is about something far more important.

Every form of harm reduction mentioned so far in this book would qualify as enabling. Take needle exchange—that's one way to make an addict's life more bearable and safer. Now, technically, anything you do to help make that addict's life more "manageable" is enabling, isn't it? Why? Because you're depriving him (or her) of the "opportunity" to learn some really cool lessons: what it's like to suffer from AIDS, run people over when you're drunk, get raped, lose your children, see your children cry, see them die. If you're an addict like me, this is the kind of stuff said to do you good. You sure do learn stuff! Yeah, and I feel sorry for anyone who doesn't experience these things. But maybe, as a corrective, everyone except addicts should enjoy these blessings for a couple of years. We really have been inconsiderate to hog it all up for ourselves.

Dealing with Addiction

So I'm thinking that if we addicts want to be good citizens, we should let others enjoy the benefits of torture and degradation. It would be good, you know, because they have a right to learn things too. They could all hit bottom, and become spiritual.

Wake up already! This is war. For over a century, larger society has been waging war on people like us. Society even manages to enlist us so that we can degrade each other, kill each other off. All the while, preachy excuses are provided. No one has to feel, or taste, what they're really doing. Think about it: it's some kind of crazy, fucked-up, feel-good genocide. But genocide with a happy face is still genocide.

You know, when I was visiting that woman in the hospital, I fell in love. She did, too. Prior to a deterioration of her condition, a full recovery from all the paralysis was supposedly imminent. We were planning a life together. We had a connection before, and I think I would have tracked her down in the hood anyway, but that's hypothetical. This is not: for a few short weeks, we were soul mates. Maybe we still are. I don't know. I was clean, strong, and confident. She was weak, and paralyzed through almost half her body. She looked up to me like some kind of hero, a savior, and I must confess that I didn't discourage it. Maybe I should have. Maybe I was a punk for letting it play out that way. Too bad: I was set to help her get out and stay out. I felt good. We both did. I once told her something like the following: "This demon took away my dignity, my self-respect, and it has made my mother cry. It burned me and made me feel like a waste of skin. But I'm back! And I'll be buried in rat shit before I let this monster take you out!" I meant it, and she looked at me with big, trusting eyes. Then the condition got worse. What now, tough guy?

Well, it all left me paralyzed for a while. But I'm not paralyzed now. I am stronger, and more focused, than ever before. If I can turn her death, and that of many others, into a victory of some kind, then maybe it'll all make sense. Or, maybe it'll just seem a little less stupid. Anyway, I have to try.

Here's something you, dear reader, ought to think about: this woman did not die because people were told to stop enabling her. By trying to manage her addiction, cut back and mitigate the harm at every step, she was "enabling" herself. No hanging off an enabler here—just self-help. Then someone I've never met, an addict in recovery, convinced her to stop enabling her own behavior: *don't bother trying to cut back or control; let the addiction hurt you as much as it wants to hurt you. Don't fight back. You'll be far better off if you let the demon torture you in high gear.* One addict saying that to another, doing that to another!

Remember what I told you in the introduction: crackheads like us, junkies like us—we're struggling with a demon that wants to take us out. But it's not kind enough to kill us fast. It wants to rape us, bleed us, degrade us, make our loved ones cry, take away our dignity, and then, very slowly, suck us dry.

Don't let the bastard win. Above all, don't let anyone tell you that this demon is right to torture you. You won't become better, and you won't become enlightened, because somebody shoves a sharp, rusty pipe up your ass. If anyone suggests that you will, tell him to try it on himself and that you'd prefer to learn through observation.

We must stop doing this to each other! We need to start taking care of each other, helping each other at every step, even when the addiction is active—especially then, because that's when we're in trouble and really need a hand. How's this: I'll help you right now when you're fucked, and if I ever fall, you can return the favor. We need to stop listening to a propaganda machine that has convinced us to degrade each other instead. I have a vision: 20 years from now, it might not matter if others—spouses, relatives, and so on—refuse to enable my people. If we start to enable ourselves, that'll be plenty. People who don't manage to abstain don't have to be sidelined. They can be integrated and encouraged to do their best.

Another vision: considerably more people achieving long-term abstinence because we start doing the exact opposite of what the bottoming out pushers have been suggesting. How much more abstinence will that generate? Hard to say. Will it add to the totals? Definitely, because nothing could be less effective than the idiotic hit bottom philosophy we've inherited from the 20th century.

What about tough love? Most of the guys who advocate "tough love" aren't man enough to be my girlfriend. Still, sometimes I'm really tempted to do them a favor.

The following chapter will explain how, and why, our degradation began.

Dealing with Addiction

It's war, you know
It's genocide
They kill us off
They bleed us dry

We even thank them
And soon you'll know
How it all took off
You'll know why

7

How this nonsense all started—a bit of history that everyone should know

If I personally identify with many targeted groups, perhaps most notably people of African descent, there's a reason for it. I'm not any stupid wannabe. It was in the early 20th century that addicts like me were starting to get it. Well, black people had long been the main target. So, much of what was applied to them could be changed just a little and used on us. No matter how oversimplified, this gives you a decent nutshell—one that I'd like you to keep in mind throughout this chapter.

This is also the most difficult chapter in the book. I cover a great deal of history in a short space. I try to keep it clear, but I ask you also to make an effort to keep up. As always, I'm not interested in talking down to my readers. If you want to learn more, read up—all the sources you need to get started are right at the end.

It was just over 200 years ago that what we call "addiction" was discovered. Oh, struggles with temptation had long been understood. So in a more general sense, people had long had some awareness of how booze, sex, or whatever might take someone over. The habit gets strong, and then it's as though a person can't stop. But an intense, focused, and large-scale concern with people being out of control was new. Many factors came into play, converging in the creation of the stereotypical addict—the fuckup we all know today.

In an individualistic culture, full of self-starters and very concerned with liberty and individuality, *the lack of self-control,* the lack of personal freedom, was very problematic. People who couldn't control themselves weren't really "free," so addiction was basically an insult to everything that American/capitalist culture wanted people to be.

The emerging needs of industrialization were also key. Complex factories, for example, needed workers who weren't tripping over themselves. On the old farm, it might not have mattered so much, but this was a different world, requiring a new breed of worker. Such a world also required savvy citizens, responsible business people, and so on. An intense kind of self-control, one that most old-school aristocrats needed only at certain times, was now expected day to day.

There was also a process of medicalization. You see, many issues that had been dealt with by priests were now being dealt with more and more by medical people. So although same-sex coupling had long been considered a sin, it was being transformed into a "disease" (more recently, of course, it came to be viewed as an acceptable lifestyle). Anyway, sins were being transformed into diseases, and chronic drunkenness didn't escape that trend.

Alcohol was troublesome, drunkenness more so, and since alcohol was the most common substance of abuse, it also became the first standard for substance addiction. To this day, the ways in which we understand cocaine and heroin addiction are indebted to these first forays into what is now called "alcoholism."

Strong religious currents were also in the picture. Not just because of America's puritan roots, but also because of issues surrounding free will, divine grace, and foreknowledge. Now, North Americans were big on religion. It seemed that people wanted two things in the Land of the Free: money and salvation. While people might not have been very philosophical, many understood debates over the nature of free will with a fair bit of sophistication. There's a reason for that. Methodism and (to a lesser extent) Baptism were essentially reactions to Calvinism (typically Presbyterian and Congregationalist) and the doctrine of predestination. Often two neighboring towns that might have seemed very similar to you or me were separated by subtle distinctions in their understanding of free will and its role in the reception of divine grace. The difference was important to people at the time because everyone knew that members of that other town were going to hell. So free will was a big issue, one that even poorly educated Americans might spend time talking about.

Take the themes just listed: it all made for a climate very well suited to talk about free will in relation to addiction: how come these people don't seem to have free will when they drink? Why can't they stop?

The anti-alcohol Temperance movement was North America's single biggest mass movement ever. There's been nothing like it before or since. I want to give you a sense of how mixed up—

downright screwy—things could be. Many 19th century slaveholders, even though they drank themselves, supported Temperance because they saw alcohol as a *disinhibitor* likely to foster rebellion among blacks. Many black leaders supported Temperance because they saw alcohol as a *pacifier*, likely to quell political action among their people. So, with respect to this matter, those two guys could be on the same side. I shit you not.

Now, during the 19th century, alcohol was the big problem. Opiates received attention but were not considered nearly as harmful. Later in the 19th century, cocaine became popular, but it was socially acceptable. You might have heard that Coca-Cola originally contained cocaine. Blow was OK. Booze was not.

During most of the 19th century, your typical opiate user was white, middle class, and female. She could have been hooked, but it might not have mattered too much because opiates were cheap and easy to get. This all started to change after more Chinese immigrants began to settle on the West coast. Their drug of choice was opium, and mostly they worked building railroads. When an economic depression rendered much of their labor superfluous, and made it harder for white, unionized workers to get jobs, anti-Chinese sentiment became rampant. At least in the New World, that's when opiates really started to be viewed as evil. Racist sentiment had everything to do with it.

For assorted reasons, cocaine was also becoming less respectable and more likely to be associated with minorities and the underclass. One important catalyst emerged in the South at the dawn of the 20th century. Cocaine had become the drug of choice for many southern blacks who had been deprived of alcohol due to local prohibitory statutes. Cocaine originally became popular not just as a stimulant, but also as a cure for certain ailments such as sinusitis. It was also used as a "cure" for addictions to opium, morphine, and alcohol. However, at a time marked by lynchings, segregation laws, and the disempowerment of blacks in general, *Negroes on cocaine* were said to attack whites, rape whites, and even to possess the ability to withstand .32 caliber bullets. As the story goes, this is why Florida state troopers switched to .38s at the time. It's hard to prove that this was the reason for the switch, but the timing fits and (in my opinion) it's the best explanation we have.

According to David Musto, who before his recent death was the world's top authority on these historical currents:

> So far, evidence does not suggest that cocaine caused a crime wave but rather that anticipation of black rebellion inspired white alarm. Anecdotes often told of superhuman strength, cunning, and efficiency resulting from cocaine. One of the most terrifying beliefs about cocaine was that it actually improved pistol marksmanship. Another myth, that cocaine made blacks almost unaffected by mere .32 caliber bullets, is said to have caused southern police departments to switch to .38 caliber revolvers. These fantasies characterized white fear, not the reality of cocaine's effects, and gave one more reason for the repression of blacks ... (Musto, 1973, p. 7)

None of this is meant to suggest that cocaine and opiates are harmless, just that racism had a lot to do with an emerging hostility toward drugs that had been socially acceptable till then. To get a sense of the situation, note that till sometime in the early 20th century, opiate addiction was explained like this: the opium smoker (or morphine injector) is much like the drunkard—he can't stop. By the mid-20th century, it was the other way around: people had to be told that alcoholics were a lot like junkies, and that's why they couldn't stop. By then, all addictions were understood by reference to the junkie—derelict, scumbag—but it took a lot of history to get us there.

So, how did these scumbags come to be? Well, as certain drugs became less and less acceptable, they were increasingly indulged in by those on the fringes of acceptability. When the typical opiate addict was a little white lady who went to church and baked cookies, it was impossible to tell the public that addicts were all liars, thieves, and derelicts. Here's something you need to know: *how any addiction is perceived will depend upon who is addicted.* As long as the typical cocaine injector in the public mind was a figure such as Sherlock Holmes, no one would believe horrible stories about cocaine addicts in general. Some may have been liars and thieves, but they couldn't all be. When the typical cocaine user was more likely to be a black person, word soon went out that all cocaine users were scum. When the typical opiate user was Chinese, opiate users were quickly perceived as conniving, back-stabbing little fucks.

Slowly but surely, as certain drugs became less acceptable, the people who would use them were more likely to be underclass: criminals, rebels, racial minorities—whoever. Slowly, the addict was being transformed into a criminal. Obviously, addicts became more and more likely to lie about their addiction. It was becoming less acceptable, so they were more inclined to hide it. After drug prohibition, prices went up, so people had to do whatever they could to support their habits. Some psychiatrists could, quite honestly, write books about opiate addiction and how the disease "causes" one to become a liar and a thief. The same "science" would have been a joke back when your typical opiate addict was probably too scared of God to even lie about having eaten the last cookie.

Things were changing fast. More and more, fucked-up white boys (like me) would come to represent addiction as such. *You didn't have to be black, or Asian, to have an identity thrust upon you that was originally rooted in prejudice against those groups.* OK, other groups, too—I'm trying to cover a lot of ground here.

To make a very, very long story short: through the 19th century, addictions were understood through a more benign kind of science. Since they targeted respectable elements, and since the main drug was alcohol, which was well-known to the public and hard to demonize, judgmental attitudes had to be tapered. Oh, there were many harsh accounts, in some ways downright nasty, but for the most part, studies of what was often called "inebriety" contained at least some balance. This first started to change when the typical addict was less and less likely to be white or middle class.

There was also a drive for prohibition, first of alcohol and later of drugs such as opiates and cocaine. This also made for more condemnation and a lot less sympathy. More and more, the "science" surrounding drug addiction began to paint the typical addict as a liar, a thief, and a psychopath with no moral center—basically someone completely out of control and with no regard for the wellbeing of others. To repeat: this kind of science would have seemed ridiculous back when most respectable citizens at least knew someone—a nice old aunt, a school teacher—with a strong opium habit. Ditto with cocaine—when quite a few doctors and professors used it because it made them feel smart, and told others to do the same, bad images of cocaine users wouldn't have the same credibility.

Dealing with Addiction

Now, for this crackhead, *the most important part of the whole development was the role played by addicts themselves.* A reformed opium user might want to put distance between herself and her habit, and might want to garner sympathy. So she might tell anyone who would listen what a liar and a cheat she had been. A good person at first, while in the addiction, she could not be trusted. Or, an early 20th century journalist might claim that he was able to get an interview with a wanted criminal shortly after having become an opium smoker. Now possessing the mind of a criminal, he knew where that criminal would hide. *Addicts themselves, at every step, were active in their own demonization.* No matter how silly some of the stories might have been, the public lapped it up. To a lesser extent, medical and other professionals also bought it. This became more common once the drugs had become illegal. More and more, lying and cheating went with a habit, and more and more people thought that the habit was the only cause. *Of course, it helped that addicts often played along.*

In such a climate, where addicts were basically seen as pure liars, psychopathic misfits who didn't give a shit about anything except getting high, the idea that only total degradation could make a real difference became easier to swallow. *This is how the current attitude about needing to bottom out got started.* Of course there's more to it, and I can't cover it all right here. Alcoholism was also addressed with bottoming-out stories, even though drunks were not painted with quite the same brush. Recall, however, that only a few decades before alcohol had been the main demon. Drunkards were in the process of becoming more acceptable than junkies, but when Bill Wilson and the first AAs started their journey, they were coming out of a culture that demonized alcohol, too. So there was some of that going on at different levels, and in many different ways.

Despite all the complexity, a few things should be clear:

1. Only a setting in which addicts are perceived as pure scumbuckets could generate an idea that complete degradation, maybe even beatings and torture, could somehow be good for them. This is where the nonsense about needing to hit bottom got off the ground.
2. These perceptions were specific to a certain time and place, and would have been considered insane only a few decades before. It all came down to history, context, politics, and timing.

3. For their own self-serving reasons, addicts often played along. So it's not fair just to blame society—we addicts have long been a part of the process that makes it OK to kick us around. Obviously, the solution will have to involve taking some responsibility.

Fast forward to the present. An addict in recovery might tell people that only an addict can ever understand another addict. While there might be a little bit of truth to this, such statements make addicts feel very clever, insightful, and in possession of some kind of strange power. Of course, we addicts possess no strange powers, and telling the world that we do simply makes us all look like a bunch of weird monsters with scary abilities. If that were true, society might be right to keep us down and to deprive us of all liberty. "You can't con a con!" may sound good, but it's obviously nonsense. Anyone can be played, even if some are harder to play than others. This kind of chatter might make some addicts feel good about themselves, but it's a wad of crap. As well, exaggerating how horrible and evil your thoughts and actions were while you were using might make you feel as though you are putting distance between yourself and that world. *But you are also telling the rest of the world that you are not a human being like others, but some kind of unnatural abomination.*

The entire recovery culture currently in practice—from treatment centers to the rooms of 12 Step groups—still participates in this process. It will do no good to expect society to stop mystifying addicts, demonizing addicts, as long as the addicts play it up and encourage society to perceive them that way.

There, you have the history. You know how it all started. You have been enlightened about your role in a process that has long justified your degradation.

Take some responsibility.

Time to wake up.
Time to get busy.
Time to step up.
Make 'em go tizzy.

8

The meaning of addiction—there's more to it than dependence

There are so many ways to define addiction that it's hard to decide where to start. I will focus on one issue, the misunderstanding of which has caused more harm than any other definitional wrangle: addiction is not just dependence. There is much more to it than that. We depend on air, food, water, and many things. Nothing wrong with that, even if today's *me* culture permits some addiction counselors to make statements such as the following: "I don't want to depend on anything outside of myself, and you shouldn't either." OK, moron, do us all a favor and stop breathing.

A bit of history is in order. In the 1980s, the people responsible for creating the *DSM* (the official *Diagnostic and Statistical Manual of Mental Disorders*) opted to use the term "dependence" instead of "addiction" for substance use disorders. Their intentions were good. At the time, addiction was such a dirty word that they wanted to avoid stigmatizing the afflicted. The previous chapter explains much of this. For the record, in the 1970s, most tobacco smokers who knew that they were hooked still didn't consider themselves addicts. Most alcoholics didn't either. But that was a different time, and the next *DSM* will likely use the term addiction. Let's hope so. Invoking dependence has really confused the issue.

The definition of *dependence* offered in the *DSM* is really an addiction model. There's more to this conception of addiction than depending on a substance, whether that's methadone or pain killers (how about insulin for diabetes?). If you do fine as long as you get what you need, there is no disorder. If, on the other hand, *getting your dose ruins your life, but not getting it also messes you up,* then there is a real concern. People don't go to treatment or to meetings just because they depend on a drug. If the drugs are working for them, they might as well keep using them. If the drugs stop working, and someone also realizes that quitting seems impossible—only then does it make sense to speak of addiction. If you can live with it, you're fine. If you can live without it, you're fine. If you can't live with it, and can't live without it, you're in trouble.

That is the only definition of addiction that matters. People can preach, for example, about how methadone, antidepressants, and a range of other substitutes are still drugs. Well, some don't do well with these substitutes, so maybe that's a problem. Others do very well, sometimes for 20 years or more, and that's only a problem if preachy interlopers turn it into one. Same for an ex-junkie who drinks beer at baseball games—people who take issue with such things do far more harm than good.

To repeat: anyone who thinks that dependence is the problem might have to conclude that we are all air addicts, food addicts, and water addicts. Maybe we are. So what? The same applies to all the things we depend upon, from sunshine to gravity. We depend upon other people as well. That's natural: everyone needs love, everyone needs company. So a relationship of any kind is not unhealthy simply because two individuals depend on each other. By that standard, of course, all relationships would be sick (and self-help gurus would keep getting rich). If some kind of interdependence is causing undue stress or unhappiness, that may be an issue. As such, however, emotional dependence is perfectly natural. And only a civilization reared on cowboy flicks and other extreme expressions of independence would be stupid enough to tell people that they should not depend on others for contentment, love, fulfillment, and recognition. Now, if you actually know someone who feels no need for that, then there's a pathological condition worth exploring.

Many themes come into a broader conception of addiction, a definition that can help people rather than cause more harm.

1. Craving is important—addicts often crave something that they know will do them harm. However, if whatever you crave will not do you harm, then, again, there's no disorder to deal with. Just take what you need. Whether that's air, a pain killer, or something else, there's no disorder worth mentioning.

2. Obsession—addicts often obsess on their drug. That can happen even if they get all the drugs they want. If someone

on methadone doesn't obsess as long as his or her requirements are being met, then the solution might be to meet those requirements.

3. Loss of control—addicts seemingly can't stop even if they want to. The key term is "want to." If someone can't stop, but doesn't want to stop, that's not an issue. I can't stop breathing for more than a very short time, but I'm cool with that. It's important to be clear on this matter: *not being able to give something up is only a problem if you experience a real need to give it up.*

4. Dysfunction, tragedy, turmoil—these are important. If what you are doing isn't messing up your life, or the lives of those around you, then nobody has a right to tell you not to keep it up.

Now back to dependence. We all depend on things. It's a part of what we are. Beyond things like air and water, we depend on each other. We need each other for love and belonging, and we also need each other economically: human society has from the start involved different people performing different tasks. No member of society does it all for himself. Yes, your cowboy movies lied to you. So did the codependency movement.

If we are to tackle the addiction issue properly, there must be no ambiguity on two points:

1. Addiction is a problem.
2. Dependence is irrelevant.

9

Recovery from addiction—time to get serious about what that means

Let's start by clearing the air. Recovery involves improvement. A partial recovery, or ongoing incremental recovery, is still recovery. This is true for all illnesses, and addictions are no different. If recovery must be associated with "sobriety," then a more flexible and realistic conception of sobriety will be required. Why should someone who smokes marijuana once in a while be excluded from a realistic conception of recovery? What if this person used to smoke crack, get into fights, and drive drunk? I'd call a switch to one joint a week commendable. A common problem involves confusion over two notions: sobriety and recovery. The first, by definition, is a state. The second is a process. If someone who once abused drugs every day is now abusing them only once a week, that would be a serious improvement. The person may not be cured, but seems to be recovering—*which really means "getting better."* What we don't need is a conception of recovery that may in some ways suit those within 12 Step fellowships, and those inside of abstinence-based treatment programs, but ignores the larger picture: a vast majority of addicts who change their lives do not fit this mold. And even within the treatment systems and the 12 Step fellowships, the numbers are few. So this pure abstinence model merely suits the imaginations—the pipedreams—of people in the treatment business and the 12 Step world. It doesn't reflect reality. It's an illusion, a smokescreen. If an addict has made major advances, taken steps in positive directions that few would argue with, then it is absurd to suggest that this person is not recovering. A switch from 10 bottles or 10 bags a week to 2 bottles or 2 bags a week is a *huge* improvement and obviously should qualify as "recovery."

Above all, perhaps, it is important to think of recovery as something that starts well before involvement in treatment or self-help groups. Contrary to all the nonsense you've heard about hitting bottom, most people improve well before engaging with those systems. Stopping and starting, slowing down, correcting bad behaviors—it's a process.

Much of the insistence on pure abstinence is based on the delusion that we have the ability to just make it happen. No matter what you've been told, the effectiveness of treatment, AA, and other 12 Step fellowships is still a question mark. Retention rates are low, and long-term abstinence is rare. When it does occur, we still have no way of determining, in any one case, if recovery would have occurred anyway. Unassisted, so-called natural recovery is well documented and accounts for more cases than those associated with 12 Step fellowships and formal treatment combined. Now, if well over 90 percent of those accessing treatment, as well as newcomers to AA, NA, or CA, resume drinking or drugging within the first year, what are we left with? The available approaches are deemed effective because we count only the minority—I repeat, quite possibly individuals who would have changed their ways with or without addiction treatment, 12 Steps, and other available interventions. Here's how success is created in the minds of believers: successes count, failures don't, hence success rates of 100 percent by definition. It is easy to say that "The program never fails. People fail the program." Still, given the current state of knowledge, it would be far more realistic to describe 12 Step approaches, along with other approaches offered by professionals, as *helpful* rather than *effective*. They can give you a nudge, but that's all. Without this kind of humility, the helping professions will not achieve a realistic perspective on their own efforts—and that is precisely what will be required if realistic goals are to be set. A good definition of recovery can't be based on delusions.

Some people have even begun to suggest that smoking cigarettes is inconsistent with recovery. Instead of opening up the space so that real people in the real world can find their way, puritanical currents are out to shrink the terrain. Are we to take seriously the idea that a compulsive gambler who once swindled money from parents, employers, and others, and is now turning it around and paying off debts and living honestly, should be deprived of recovery status because he or she still smokes cigarettes? Should this apply to someone who till recently smoked crack and got drunk every day? My friends in GA and NA would, quite justifiably, take issue. First things first, as they say in the rooms.

Let's recap something already covered in Chapter 2. There are many ways to relapse, such as sexually acting out, gambling irresponsibly, and abusing people verbally and physically—the list is endless. Any of these is just as unhealthy as drug abuse. Now, only 1 in 20 who enter the system manage to abstain completely from booze and dope for two straight years. Of those, how many refrain from *all behavioral relapse* over that time? Let's start with 1,000 people. Fifty of 1,000 (1 in 20) are clean from substances. Of those 50, how many really abstain from *all* maladaptive behaviors? I'd say none, but what if it's 3? We are left with a conception of "recovery" that only 3 of 1,000 will ever achieve. What about the other 997? The game is rigged to make sure that almost everyone loses. So here's the choice: we can side with 997 people, or with a stupid idea. If we'd rather side with humanity, then the abstinence principle must go.

Recall too that all substitute drug therapies can be derided because of their inconsistency with "abstinence." Now, please recall how I label *codependency*. Well, that's not the only "stupid word that doesn't mean anything." *Abstinence* can be just as bad.

In other ways, too, an uncompromising commitment to simple ideas about abstinence leads to an overlooking of reality, and very obvious reality at that. By simply focusing on current length of clean time, recovery pushers leave us with the following scenario: someone who had been sober for 20 years and then had a slip six months ago would now be in the early stage of recovery, supposedly less advanced than someone who was using daily throughout the same two decades and then sobered up a year ago. Are we really to believe that, from a developmental point of view, the second person is likely to be in better shape than the first? Any expert who makes this claim should have his credentials revoked. So even if one wanted to stick to an abstinence principle (not a good idea), a more meaningful way to measure abstinence would be to count total number of clean days over, say, the last decade or even the last year. If clean time is to be a marker, the measure simply cannot be someone's most recent cutoff date. People heal over years, and a few slips along the way need not put them back to square. It is one thing for informal, 12 Step fellowships to measure things this way. But we can, and should, expect more from professionals.

A final note: illegal acts can—in some cases—be consistent with recovery. Many make the following point: drugs are illegal, so blah,

blah, blah ... Not very convincing, is it? *First a few queries:* if marijuana and LSD were legal, could their use be consistent with recovery? In settings where gambling is illegal, is a low bet and perfectly controlled card game with one's friends inconsistent with recovery? When homosexuality was illegal, was practicing gay sex inconsistent with recovery? America has a long tradition of disobedience, starting perhaps with the Boston Tea Party and running through the Underground Railroad, to a host of more recent developments that even the most conservative among us have come to accept as legitimate. *The point is not that we should treat the law with disrespect, but that it takes more than legal sanction to make an act inconsistent with recovery.*

I am not here to tell the world what recovery has to mean. My point, precisely, is that it can mean different things to different people. Pure abstinence would be necessary for someone "recovering" from violent behavior, and maybe even for a gambler capable of playing away a family home over a weekend. Again, a drug addict or alcoholic with such problems might want to invoke pure abstinence from those behaviors more vehemently than with substance use. What matters most is this:

1. If it's *your recovery,* then only you can say what recovery means. People in the system are consultants, not boot camp leaders, football coaches, or gurus of any kind. They are not your baby sitter, and they are not the ones who can tell you what to think, how to speak, what to eat, or when to have sex. Above all: you need to decide for yourself which behaviors and substances you want to drop.

2. If it's *our recovery,* then addicts everywhere should have a hand in defining the parameters. The small minority of abstainers in self-help groups should not have the last word. Over the next few decades, together, we might generate some great ideas about what recovery ought to mean. But that can only happen if we open our ears, open our eyes, and open our minds. Real knowledge is needed, preferably scientific, but at least not ridiculous. We can quibble over definitions and exchange ideas. One thing, though, is certain: the abstinence pushers offer nothing but illusions, and very harmful illusions at that.

3. It would be hard to come up with a conception of "recovery" that is more unsound—more stupid, more harmful—than the one we inherited from the 20th century.

Time to leave it in the dust.

10

Odds and ends—things that we can do without

The matters discussed in this section are mainly political, and inroads into recovery issues are a spin-off. When women started stepping up, when blacks started stepping up—job one was putting an end to being spoken to, and treated, as though you were a child. The snippets below were written to clear the air, and they may also serve as a *how to manual* for responding to people who talk nonsense or try to belittle you. Special attention is paid to addiction treatment because that is a setting wherein addicts are vulnerable and easier to push around, and also because it is in early recovery that addicts are often trained to think in ways that belittle them—and other addicts everywhere—by means of an insidious process of infantilization.

- Kicking people out of treatment—*try not to, on principle*

A friend of mine who read an earlier draft of this book was once turfed from treatment for playing too much cribbage in his spare time. Would a hospital refuse to fix someone's broken leg because they don't approve of that person's behavior? Well, if we are to take addiction seriously as a medical condition, then we should think clearly. Now, it can't be the same with a behavioral disorder. Violence and other forms of disruption have to be curtailed. Still, every effort should be made to take a client-centered approach. And every type of Nazi-ass boot camp logic, along with *any* attempt to impose one's beliefs and values on clients, must stop. A principle that has long applied to medical practice should be applied right here: I may not like racism or some other forms of bigotry. Someone else might not like gays or my dirty fucking mouth. But neither I, nor "someone else," would have a right to refuse a kidney operation to anyone because of such things. It really is that simple. No matter how strongly we feel about an issue, we don't impose our values on patients. We don't use our position of power and authority to that end—ever. The same should apply if the patient is struggling with drug addiction. Period.

- If you really wanted to get better, you'd stick it out—*sorry, but that depends*

You might hear talk about someone leaving a detox or treatment facility because of a stupid rule. Take not even being allowed to step out for a smoke. Often, people say that if the person really wanted to kick, he or she would have stuck it out. First, that's not necessarily true—sometimes a nic-fit makes kicking really unbearable. More importantly, there is a principle at stake. Consider how this line of thinking can be used to justify anything: if you really wanted to kick, you'd put up with a smack in the mouth, sexual harassment, or whatever. Maybe you would. Maybe you wouldn't. That's not the issue. A rule—any rule—should require better justification than that. And when addicts themselves pay lip service to that line of thinking, they have basically said that how addicts are treated is irrelevant. Try this: *If you really wanted recovery, you wouldn't leave just because a counselor kicked you in the nuts*. Even if that were true, it wouldn't make it OK. Think about how addicts have actually been trained to buy into a line of reasoning that could, in principle, justify any degradation heaped upon them. Again, a rule should require more than such lame justification—and it's another example of the kind of simplistic and patronizing tripe that has governed addictions for far too long. Sure, if I really want to kick, I might be willing to cut off one of my fingers. It's such a stupid point, and who would dare talk this way to any other marginalized group? If you really wanted equality, you'd put up with ... yeah, sure.

- No smoking during substance abuse treatment—*I'll make my own decisions, thank you*

Since we just touched on the topic of smoking: you might hear that preventing you from stepping out and having a smoke when you're kicking other drugs has been proven to be beneficial. Well, studies have shown that the old line—"Don't even think about quitting smoking during the first year"—is nonsense. Many give it all up at once, and that's great. However, these things are person-specific—meaning that kicking tobacco right off helps some and hurts others (how could everyone be the same?). This is just another case of people in the system—preachy people, bossy people—overstepping. In a nutshell: good research is being misused.

- Please speak from the "I"—*please don't tell us how to speak!*

I don't know where this started, but often the stated purpose is to stop people from imposing their views on others. It's also a play: "I'm not telling you what to do, but in my experience ..." Of course you're being told what to do! We need a recovery culture where telling others what to do, if needed, should be done openly. What can be more pathetic than telling people what to do by pretending not to? Besides, there's a lot more to good communication than personal stories and anecdotes. That stuff has a place, but it's just plain idiotic—and patronizing—to insist that people limit themselves to that and nothing else. The idea should be to help someone with an addiction problem, not tell them how to speak, which is one step away from telling them what to think (they do that, too, don't they?). I'll make it simple. Tackling addictions requires more than experiential accounts. Though important, self-referential accounts are limited, and there is an equally important need for the kind of communication that *rises above the personal.* You know, the kind in which we engage once we're no longer toddlers? Stick to personal perspective, experience, without ever taking responsibility for talking like a grown-up? They tell you to do that, and then rip you for being childish. Just another play ...

- No "buts" please! —*why not?*

Dealing with Addiction

What kind of communication can we have if someone's suggestions can't be questioned? Why do the recovery pushers consider the word "but" on the part of a newbie to be a sign of bad attitude? See above: *please don't tell me how to speak!*

- No sex or relationships during the first year of abstinence—*again, don't let anyone infantilize you*

Are all addicts who are recently clean, or still using, too juvenile or messed up to make decent decisions about friendships and partnerships? Of course not, though some might be—and the latter is true for many with 10 years' clean and for persons who've never had a substance use disorder. First, many addicts, alcoholics, and others will never get a year of abstinence even if they do get their lives together. Plus, again, we shouldn't be infantilizing people for trying to deal with their drug problems. Will a vast majority of new entries who partner up in early recovery be gone soon? Yes, and the same applies to those who keep their legs crossed. There is no evidence that one group is less successful in the long run. Here's what you get: when someone in the "sex/relationship" group does poorly, many will claim that intimacy was the cause. However, when the same happens to a member of the chastity group, other causes are put forward. All of this has more to do with interpreting the evidence than with simply letting the facts speak. I'll give you three reasons for this prejudice: (1) The *me* culture thinks that isolation is better than connection; (2) there is a strong puritanical current at work; and (3) the entire treatment/recovery scene is dominated by individuals who want to feel superior to you, so they treat you like a child. It might not help that someone used to be where you are—very often the recovering people are more condescending to clients than the shrinks and other pros. A sad state of affairs: we addicts no longer need "others" to keep us down. We've been trained to take over the task.

- No sex among clients—*suggest that if you like, but don't make it an order*

Doctors rarely tell hospital patients what to do, or who to fool around with (!) in their spare time. Yet, quite often, people in treatment for addictions are immediately infantilized. Even in their spare time, they can't do this, they can't do that. If you think these restrictions are necessary, go to Western Europe. While some centers over there still operate on the Neanderthal North American model, others are more enlightened. Addiction treatment there is typically less bossy and more respectful of clients. A (non-Neanderthal) European treatment center might *recommend* that clients refrain from getting intimate in their spare time, but that's all. It's not an order, and it can't be, because any decent human being knows that you don't have a right to treat adults that way! Simple. If we—addicts—want to stop being society's bitch, we will have to step up: (1) I won't let you treat me that way, and (2) I'm here to stop you from treating my fellow addicts that way. Period!

- We all have the same disease—*not necessarily, and it might not matter anyway*

Often you hear that "addiction is addiction," with the suggestion that since everyone has the "same disease" they should all be dealt with in the same fashion: the solutions are supposedly the same, and even people just getting clean (newcomers) are "all the same." First, anyone acquainted with psycho-behavioral disorders can tell you that it is possible for two individuals to exhibit similar behaviors for very different reasons—so every case of addiction to the same substance need not imply that the same process (the same underlying condition/disease) is at work. Plus, and this is key: if two people have cancer, one might respond well to chemotherapy; the other might not, and hence require something else. For a host of person-specific reasons, similar conditions are often dealt with differently—this is often the case with biological diseases, and even more so with behavioral disorders. And here's the main point: Latinos are not all the same, gays are not all the same, people in wheelchairs are not all the same—and each of these groups had to fight hard to make that point clear to larger society. Now it's our turn: so don't ever let any bigoted idiot tell you that we're all the same (even if that idiot is a fellow addict).

- The allergy theory of alcoholism/addiction

If you go to an allergy specialist, any allergy you have can be identified with a pin prick. Pollen, rabbits, whatever—it's that simple. There is no such test for alcoholism, because addictions are not allergies. If they were, they could quickly be identified, and assessment would be much simpler than is still the case to this day. Does this issue matter? Well, given that many in the recovery world cling stubbornly to AA lore, it can matter. For the record, the allergy theory of alcoholism was *never* taken seriously by science or by any medical body. Put forward by W. D. Silkworth in the 1930s, the idea became a popular myth. It helped to give alcoholism a disease status among many members of the public, so Silkworth did some good with his theory. But today the notion does more harm than good, because we need to let go of the past and all the nonsense that went with it. Is alcoholism a disease? Yes, but it's not an allergy. You might have heard this one: "An allergy is defined as an abnormal reaction ..." Well, not all abnormal reactions qualify as allergic. For example, a diabetic might react abnormally to sugar, but diabetics are not allergic to sugar—different processes are involved. In any case, allergies involve immune system responses, whereas addictions target neurological, synaptic, and other systems in the body. I'm not here to discuss the bioscience, but to point out that people who don't have a clue should either read up (do the work) or shut up. We need to get real about what addiction is.

- Treating the Big Book like gospel—*think for yourself*

Many leaders and innovators—certainly the best ones—have warned their followers never to shirk the responsibility to think for themselves: don't just follow. Later, many will respect that part of the message, but others (the narrow-minded fanatics) will not. The first AAs made it clear that no one should hang off their every word: "Our book is meant to be suggestive only. We realize we know but little. God will constantly disclose more to you and to us. Ask Him in your morning meditation what you can do each day for the man who is still sick. The answers will come, if your own house is in order" (Alcoholics Anonymous World Services, 2001, p. 164). Yet anyone familiar with AA and the 12 Step movement can tell you that some—not most—AA members consider that book to be untouchable, something that must never be questioned. Too bad if Bill W and his crew had enough sense to warn future generations against such hero worship. That Bill Wilson himself was politically savvy is evidenced by how he laid down AA's 12 Traditions. If not for that display of historical and political wisdom, AA by now might not be around. Bill understood what was at stake. He knew what can happen when leaders and heroes are admired to the point where they can never be questioned. For more insight into why so many addicts and alcoholics suffer and die needlessly, just go to an AA meeting and talk to a few fanatics. Now, most AA members are not like that. But some are. Over the years, I learned a great deal from AA and NA members. Ironically, talking to nut-jobs in the 12 Step movement taught me more than talking to the others.

- Religious versus spiritual—*a contrived distinction*

The treatment industry is packed full of people telling you that their programs are spiritual, but not religious. First, *religious* is an adjective, not a noun. Try: Bobby is sloppy (adjective); Bobby is a slob (noun). The second descriptor is final, the first simply indicates tendencies. So, a practice can be *religious* without being *a religion*. For example, if people get together and pray, it is a religious practice even if they aren't all praying to the same god. Any activity that shares major traits with religion is religious, and with that established we can quibble over degrees: very religious, just a little religious, etc. This applies to many treatment programs and to all 12 Step fellowships. The distinction between religious and spiritual became a major issue in the middle and later 20th century for political reasons: "we're not ramming religion down your throat." Maybe, maybe not, but we should all note that the one main text that inspired Bill Wilson's journey was written by William James and titled: *The Varieties of Religious Experience*. James was an excellent scholar and had better things to do than talk flaky nonsense: *it's not religious, it's just spiritual, yeah that's it* ... Jung too, for the record, wrote about *religious experience,* and he insisted that atheists can have such experiences. If, for example, you see four whales swimming in the ocean and then four ships, and the connection overwhelms you for a split second, then you just had a "religious experience" in the Jungian sense. For Jung, deities were optional. Jung was a great scholar on religious topics, though he barely knew anything about addiction (whatever he may or may not have said about alcoholism should not be taken seriously—Jung had a big ego and was prone to shooting his mouth off).

- People simply saying what they've been trained to say—*think for yourself!*
    1. A man might say, "When I first showed up, I was full of shit." Perhaps, but you're in a fellowship or treatment center that has trained you to say that. You will get approval (even respect!) for saying that. You might even start believing that you were full of shit. But that doesn't make it true.
    2. A woman says, "I had to stop getting involved with other people. I had to start working on myself." Others nod with serious approval, because this poor lady is saying what she's been trained to say. She's saying what they all want to hear: self, self, self, me, me, me ... After a few years of that, we are told, she will have become less self-centered. Hmmmm ... What if she were to focus on caring for others right away? Oh, no, you can't do that! Why not?

The first example is "I suck and all my opinions are irrelevant." The second is "I should withdraw." Of the many stupid messages the recovery machine sends you, those two are among the most harmful.

- Your suffering has given you privileged insight—*stop taking that for granted!*

The West has a long tradition—at once ethical, spiritual, political, and philosophical—of giving special attention to victims. They are said to possess wisdom, a point of view more meaningful than that of anyone who has not been oppressed, downtrodden, and degraded. Best to be very careful with this line of thinking. This book has explained a lot about how your "experience" can be used to keep you down. Recall too, that the entire business of *hitting bottom* revolves around this nonsense: suffering—degradation, maybe torture, maybe rape—will give you a special type of wisdom that only such suffering can provide. Bullshit! I'll give you a bit more right here. In some ways, this kind of thinking is rooted in certain strands of Christian conceptions of redemption and providence. Let's be clear: not all Christians are sick enough to think that extreme suffering is good for people, but some are. More than any other author, Karl Marx gave the "oppressed have privileged insight" idea a real push in the 19th century. He said that the workers, who had been kept down by capitalism, would have special insight into how that system works. First, Marx was middle class himself, which is why he had the education and leisure to develop his ideas. Second, Marx was a sentimental fool whose writings have caused more oppression and suffering than those of any other author in human history (to his credit, Nietzsche was making fun of this line of thought over a hundred years ago).

Recall Chapter 4, where I pointed out that "anyone who has been burned, beaten, broken, spit on, and shit on by A, might not be the one who can tell you what A is about." It's crucial that you keep this in view, because *your own impressions can lead to your own oppression*—and many people will "validate" your impressions to that end. They can be hateful demagogues or well meaning flakes—either way, these people do us no good at all. OK, the left-wing ding-a-ling might feel pity or sympathy, and hence a need to validate everything you say. The right-wing ding-a-ling might just groove on malice, so he wants you to suffer because that's how you'll "learn" and "get the message." Despite that difference, each ding-a-ling is beholden to the same stupid premise. One of my favorite authors is the French socio-political historian, Michel Foucault. One of his books really got to the heart of Western penal systems—how they work, what they are really about. In that book, *Discipline and Punish,* Foucault doesn't quote inmates at all. He quotes the people who put the system together. You see, the guy at the wrong end of a whip is likely to be too fucked up by it all to give you a sober account. But the prick holding the whip just might. Think with me: those who have been injured are tempted at every turn to interpret all of reality from the perspective of that injury. So "everything" around you is about male domination, white culture, capitalism ... No. Reality doesn't work that way; it's never that easy. Foucault understood this perfectly. So he quoted the punisher, not the punished. He wanted to help prisoners, for real. But he knew that we didn't need another morality play about peoples' agony. Foucault offered up a clear account: cold, objective, calculated. You don't ever really get that from the victim, but you might get it from the victimizer. That's the ugly truth. With apologies to every victim on Earth, an ugly fact is still a fact. *To repeat: your suffering can skew your perspective, and those who want to hurt you and keep you down can use your own perspective against you.* All I'm saying is be careful.

- Ideologues who sideline biological determinants: left, right, and center—*leave your ideology at the door*

Many would like to turn addiction issues into a platform for their own politicking. It matters little whether your agenda is republican, socialist, or something else: on my turf—crackhead turf—leave your shit at the door. Two strands stand out above all: (1) moralistic types, concerned with individual behavior, who take issue with any disease conception of addiction because they want to blame the addict for being an addict; and (2) moralistic types, concerned with assorted social ills, who want to blame society for addiction's very existence. First, nobody becomes an addict on purpose. Second, addiction has been around a lot longer than capitalism, secular humanism, phallocentric discourse, or any pet peeve one may have. Of course, there's no denying a measure of individual responsibility, or the importance of social injustice to addiction-related matters. Yet certain ideologues want to associate any acknowledgement of addiction's status as a disease, with strong biological underpinnings, with their enemy. For example, I have been accused of neo-conservatism by left-wing flakes and of "Marxism" by right-wing flakes. Very well: let's pretend that a range of psycho-behavioral disorders—substance use disorder, pathological gambling, schizophrenia, bipolar, etc.—are primarily psychosocial in origin; we have come to the conclusion that genetic and other biological determinants are marginal in their importance. That conclusion could just as easily buttress a republican *family values* agenda as it could a feminist or socialist agenda. The Taliban might not mind, either, because they really don't want to let sinners (or Western culture) off the hook. This issue has less to do with ideological slant than with a penchant for waving one's big, moral finger in the air. One can legitimately quibble over the relative importance of bio factors, or whether a disease label is best. But the simple sidelining of biology, of nature itself, is exactly the kind of flaky, preachy mysticism our cause can do without—regardless of whether it comes from the religious right or the pseudo-sophisticated left.

- "Is that really a solution?"—*a stupid question: maybe it's just management*

With most difficulties in life—marriage problems, nagging injuries, stressors at work—people might find a way to render them tolerable or manageable, and then from there try to lead reasonably happy lives. Rarely are such issues solved outright, because serious problems rarely just disappear. With addictions, however, one is often confronted by such a standard: is this or that attempt to manage your situation really a solution? What is meant by "solution"? On top of abstinence, a perfect state of happiness that no one maintains indefinitely. Funny how many in recovery hail Bill W as a shining example. Poor guy was dogged by depression off and on for most of his life, and all the 12 Steps could do was help keep him off the sauce and make his life less troublesome. He was eventually able to lessen the depression's impact, though his success in this endeavor is often exaggerated in 12 Step circles. One could ask, is that really a solution? In fact, that is a "really" stupid question. Bill did his best. Of course he didn't "solve" all his problems. He simply *reduced the harm* and got on with his life.

- Cops are pigs—*no, only some, and so are many junkies and crackheads*

Now, the last thing we need is a punk-ass attitude toward authority. Some in authority are the enemy, some are not. One cop might kick your ass, another one might save your ass. Often they're the ones telling us to get it together, and I mean when we really should. If the goal is integration rather than ongoing segregation, then thinking clearly is a must: there is no reason to remain on the fringe, not for blacks, not for gays, and not for us.

- Do you believe in free will? —*what any one person believes is irrelevant, next question please*

There are so many ways to conceptualize addiction, with "loss of control" perhaps the most popular tack. "Impairment of control" has been used in scientific circles, and is clearly more accurate because at least some kind of control normally remains. If you are not comfortable with the "control" issue, if you insist on the presence of free will, you can view addiction as an "internal dispute" or an "internal conflict." Positing different sides of the self vying for supremacy need not imply a lack of choice. It simply describes addiction. There need be no shirking of responsibility involved. And, when you think about it, I actually suggest that an addict can be responsible for managing his or her addiction at every step, rather than abandoning everything to simplistic ideas about complete loss of control, hitting a bottom, and total abstinence. And one more thing: I've studied free will versus determinism as a philosopher in every way conceivable, as a historian of how the idea has played out over the ages, and also as a scholar of addiction. Plus I've been a drunk and a crackhead stuck with trying to figure it all out. Frankly, if I still can't fully wrap my head around this question, then the rest of humanity doesn't stand a chance.

- Recovery is a miracle—*no, it's patient labor and quite natural*

There was a time when miracles were rare and precious. An entire generation might consider itself blessed because one miracle occurred. Today, every little bit of seeming intervention might be designated as miraculous. In recovery circles, every clean day might be described as miraculous. Often, people seem to experience three or four "miracles" on their way to work: "I'm running late but the bus came early—praise the Lord!"; "My lighter doesn't work, but I found a pack of matches!" Now, I don't deny the presence of intervention. Not that it should matter, but for the record, I believe we experience it regularly. But we do ourselves little good by pretending that growing out of our addictions is special when, in fact, it's normal. Plus, every day can't be Christmas, and we really need a more serious recovery culture. What would happen if Moses were to part a sea, or if Mohammed were to move a mountain? I doubt we could call either event simply a miracle, because our culture has ruined the word. Perhaps we'd call it a Super Miracle, or a New Improved Special Miracle. And to the point: no matter how powerful someone's addiction may be, a long-term process of reduction that may or may not lead to abstinence is perfectly natural, has been occurring since the dawn of history, and it is high time we stop giving credit to fake medicine ("treatment") and religious hocus pocus. The best practitioners, the honest ones, will tell you that all they can do is give a nudge or a tweak to a process that is all yours. Of course they help, but they typically have some humility and good sense. If you get clean, or if you simply reduce substantially, it's your recovery, the function of a natural process—and you don't owe it to any institution or to any so-called spiritual crap that someone wants to sell you.

But if it's miracles you want, I'll tell you a story—all true. Once, in the middle of a crack run, I vaguely recalled that some friends were counting on me. I was expected to show up, and possibly there would be violence. The idea was that violence would be much less likely if I were there, but it could happen either way. I'm not one to let my friends down, but I was in a haze: sexual ideation, craving more dope, barely cognizant. I had lots of dope and plenty of money. How to stop? This might have been the hardest thing I ever had to do. Somehow, I reached inside my soul, then I clenched my fists. I let out a shout, and focused my mind on who was counting on me and what might happen if I didn't show. Quickly I threw cold water on my face, threw all my shit down the toilet, and guzzled enough OJ to almost make me barf. I nuked some really strong, gross coffee and sucked it back. I went, I walked, sobering up with every step. I showed up and did what had to be done. I wasn't 100 percent, but I came through. Still, when I think back to how close I came to letting down my crew, I must confess that I could have easily lost that struggle. Now, that would have been a miracle.

11

Postscript

I wrote this book to lay down the truth. I want to make a difference for so many others like myself: the junkies, the crackheads, the fuckups—the scum and the filth. If we want to stop being perceived this way, it'll have to start with how we perceive ourselves. No sense expecting larger society to respect you until you really start to respect yourself. No sense expecting larger society to stop kicking you around until you stop telling the world that people like you have it coming.

If you get nothing else out of this book, get this: drug addiction is, first and foremost, not a recovery issue, a moral issue, or a public health issue. Oh, it's all of those things—but above all, it's a political issue. Like gays, blacks, and others, addicts need a political center. We need to back each other. We need to organize—yes, that's right. Time was, nobody would have thought that gays could do it, but they did. We can!

"Harm reduction" often serves as a catchall for any pragmatic, helpful initiative that isn't governed by uncompromising (e.g., pure abstinence) attitudes. When those attitudes become less dominant, different approaches to helping people might not even require a designation that really implies a no-brainer: let's reduce harm. Only someone who thinks that addicts ought to be harmed would take issue. With respect to addictions, we are just starting to emerge from the Dark Ages.

For years, I wanted to write something like this. One thing stopped me: I wanted to find a way to do it without giving the 12 Step movement a shiner. That was my first choice, and I will always be grateful for the love and support my many Stepper friends have given me. I love you guys, and it's not my fault you're brainwashed. Many of you are doing more harm than good out there. This book had to be written.

We, firstborn of the 21st century, have all the knowledge we need to make the coming years a bit better than the century we left behind.

In our search for justice, we really have come a long way. We no longer tell Jews, children, or gays that they ought to suffer extremes of degradation, and we don't say that to the disabled or the mentally ill. There was a time we did, but such an abusive posture is inconsistent with everything our Western civilization has been trying to accomplish for the last 200 years: freedom, justice, equity. Addicts are certainly not the only oppressed group, but when we think through how addiction is understood and dealt with, it clearly serves as a microcosm for all the injustices—and the stupidities—our civilization has been trying to leave behind. Crackheads, junkies, working girls—now it's our play, and this might just be the last frontier.

Be safe.

P

12
Further reading

Note that the titles offered deal not only with illicit drugs, but also with alcohol and a range of behavioral addictions. The literature below has been compiled to enable you to educate yourself, and to learn about addiction from a range of perspectives. Note as well that my classifications are somewhat arbitrary, and that quite a few titles could have been placed in more than one section.

a. Readiness to Change—as Opposed to Hitting Bottom

Begun, A., Murphy, C., Bolt, D., et al. (2003). Characteristics of the Safe At Home instrument for assessing readiness to change intimate partner violence. *Research on Social Work Practice, 13,* 80–107.

Bertholet, N., Horton, N., & Saitz, R. (2009). Improvements in readiness to change and drinking in primary care patients with unhealthy alcohol use: A prospective study. *BMC Public Health, 9,* 101–110.

Center for Substance Abuse Treatment (CSAT). (2009). Treatment Improvement Protocol series. Retrieved from http://tie.samhsa.gov/externals/tips.html

Dalton, C., Gottlieb, L., & Shaw, F. (2003). The concept of readiness to change. *Journal of Advanced Nursing, 42,* 108–117.

DiClemente, C. (2003). *Addiction and change: How addictions develop and addicted people recover.* New York, NY: Guilford Press.

DiClemente, C., Story, M., & Murray, K. (2000). On a roll: The process of initiation and cessation of problem gambling among adolescents. *Journal of Gambling Studies, 16,* 289–313.

Duncan, D. (1974). The acquisition, treatment and maintenance of polydrug dependence: A public health model. *Journal of Psychedelic Drugs, 7,* 209–213.

Duncan, D. (1974). Drug abuse as a coping mechanism. *American Journal of Psychiatry, 131,* 724.

Khantzian, E. (1985). The self-medication hypothesis of addictive disorders: Focus on heroin and cocaine dependence. *American Journal of Psychiatry, 142,* 1259–1264.

Khantzian, E., Mack, J., & Schatzberg, A. (1974). Heroin use as an attempt to cope: Clinical observation. *American Journal of Psychiatry, 131,* 160–164.

Khantzian, E. J. 1999. *Treating addiction as a human process.* Northvale, NJ: Jason Aronson.

Marlatt, G., Baer, J., Donovan, D., et al. (1988). Addictive behaviors: Etiology and treatment. *Annual Review of Psychology, 39,* 223–252.

Nathan, P. (2003). The role of natural recovery in alcoholism and pathological gambling. *Journal of Gambling Studies, 19,* 279–286.

Ogborne, A. (1978). *Patient characteristics as predictors of treatment outcomes for alcohol and drug abusers.* Toronto, ON: Evaluation Studies Department, Addiction Research Foundation.

Peele, S. (1989). *Diseasing of America: Addiction treatment out of control.* Lexington: Jossey Bass Books.

Slutske, W. (2006). Natural recovery and treatment-seeking in pathological gambling: Results of two U.S. national surveys. *American Journal of Psychiatry, 163,* 297–302.

Vaillant, G. (1983). *The natural history of alcoholism.* Cambridge, MA: Harvard University Press.

Zimmerman, G., Olsen, C., & Bosworth, M. (2000). A "stages of change" approach to helping patients change behavior. *American Family Physician, 61,* 1409–1416.

b. The Efficacy of Treatment—Abstinence as Just One Option Among Many

Biernacki, P. (1986). *Pathways from heroin addiction.* Philadelphia, PA: Temple University.

Birke, S., Edelmann, R., & Davis, P. (1990). An analysis of the abstinence violation effect in a sample of illicit drug users. *British Journal of Addiction, 85,* 1299–1307.

Carnes, P., Murray, R., & Charpentier, L. (2005). Bargains with chaos: Sex addicts and addiction interaction disorder. *Sexual Addiction & Compulsivity, 12,* 79–120.

Curry, S., Marlatt, G., & Gordon, J. (1987). Abstinence violation effect: Validation of an attributional construct with smoking cessation. *Journal of Consulting and Clinical Psychology, 55,* 145–149.

Day, E., & Strang, J. (2011). Outpatient versus inpatient opioid detoxification: A randomized control trial. *Journal of Substance Abuse Treatment, 40,* 56–66.

Duncan, D., Nicholson, T., Clifford, P., et al. (1994). Harm reduction: An emerging new paradigm for drug education. *Journal of Drug Education, 24,* 281–290.

Grichting, E., Uchtenhagen, A., & Rehm, J. (2002). Modes and impact of coercive inpatient treatment for drug-related conditions in Switzerland. *European Economic Research, 8,* 78–83.

Haasen, C., Verthein, U., Degkwitz, P., et al. (2007). Heroin-assisted treatment for opioid dependence: Randomised controlled trial. British *Journal of Psychiatry, 191,* 55–62.

Hall, S., Havassy, B., & Wasserman, D. (1990). Commitment to abstinence and acute stress in relapse to alcohol, opiates, and nicotine. *Journal of Consulting and Clinical Psychology, 58,* 175–181.

Horvath, A. T. (1998). Sex, drugs, gambling & chocolate: A workbook for overcoming Addictions. Cottesloe, WA: Impact Publishers.

Isbell, H. (1963). Historical development of attitudes toward opiate addiction in the United States. In S. Farber & R. Wilson (Eds.), *Man and civilization: Conflict and creativity* (pp. 154–170). New York, NY: McGraw-Hill.

Jackson-Jacobs, C. (2001). Refining rock: Practical and social features of self-control among a group of college-student crack users. *Contemporary Drug Problems, 28,* 597–622.

Keller, M. (1972). On the loss of control phenomenon in alcoholism. *British Journal of Addiction, 67,* 153–166.

Ladouceur, R., Lachance, S., & Fournier, P. (2009). Is control a viable goal in the treatment of pathological gambling? *Behaviour Research and Therapy, 47,* 189–197.

Laws, D. (1999). Relapse prevention—The state of the art. *Journal of Interpersonal Violence, 14,* 285–302.

Leslie, K. (2008). Youth substance use and abuse: Challenges and strategies for identification and intervention. *Canadian Medical Association Journal, 178,* 145–148.

MacMaster, S. (2004). Harm reduction: A new perspective on substance abuse services. *Social Work, 49,* 356–363.

Marlatt, G., & Gordon, J. (1985). *Relapse prevention: Maintenance strategies in the treatment of addictive behaviors.* New York, NY: Guilford Press.

McLellan, A., Woody, G., Metzger, D., et al. (1996). Evaluating the effectiveness of addiction treatments: Reasonable expectations, appropriate comparisons. *The Milbank Quarterly, 74,* 51–85.

Miller, W. (1992). The effectiveness of treatment for substance abuse: Reasons for optimism. *Journal of Substance Abuse Treatment, 9,* 93–102.

Miller, W. (1996). What is a relapse? Fifty ways to leave the wagon. *Addiction, 91*(12s1), 15–28.

Miller, W., Brown, T., Simpson, N., et al. (1995). What works?: A methodological analysis of the alcohol treatment outcome literature. In R. Hester & W. Miller (Eds.), *Handbook of alcoholism treatment approaches* (pp. 12–44). Boston, MA: Allyn and Bacon.

Peele, S. (1985). *The meaning of addiction.* Lexington, KY: D. C. Heath.

Peele, S. (1989). *Diseasing of America: Addiction treatment out of control.* Lexington: Jossey Bass Books.

Prendergast, M., Podus, D., Chang, E., et al. (2002). The effectiveness of drug abuse treatment: A meta-analysis of comparison group studies. *Drug and Alcohol Dependence, 67,* 53–72.

Project MATCH Research Group. (1997). Matching alcoholism treatments to client heterogeneity: Project MATCH post-treatment outcomes. *Journal of Studies on Alcohol, 58,* 7–29.

Reinarman, C. (2005). Addiction as accomplishment: The discursive construction of disease. *Addiction Research and Theory, 13,* 307–320.

Roizen, R. (1987). The great controlled-drinking controversy. In M. Galanter (Ed.), *Recent developments in alcoholism: Vol. 5. Memory deficits, sociology of treatment, ion channels, early problem drinking* (pp. 245–279). New York, NY: Plenum Press.

SAMHSA. Center for Substance Abuse Prevention (CSAP) United States. (1995). *Effectiveness of substance abuse treatment.* Rockville, MD.

Sanchez-Craig, M., & Lci, H. (1986). Disadvantages to imposing the goal of total abstinence on problem drinkers: An empirical study. *British Journal of Addiction, 81,* 505–512.

Saunders, B., & Houghton, M. (1996). Relapse revisited: A critique of current concepts and clinical practice in the management of alcohol problems. *Addictive Behaviors, 21,* 843–855.

Schaler, J. (1996). Thinking about drinking: The power of self-fulfilling prophecies. *The International Journal of Drug Policy, 7,* 187-192.

Slutske, W., Piasecki, T., Blaszczynski, A., et al. (2010). Pathological gambling recovery in the absence of abstinence. *Addiction, 105,* 2169–2175.

Sobell, M., & Sobell, L. (1972). *Individualized behavior therapy for alcoholics: Rationale, procedures, preliminary results and appendix* (Monograph No. 13). Sacramento, CA: Department of Mental Hygiene.

Sobell, M., & Sobell, L. (1976). Second year treatment outcome of alcoholics treated by individualized behavior therapy. *Behavioral Research and Therapy, 14,* 195–215.

Sobell, L., Sobell, M., & Toneatto, T. (1992). Recovery from alcohol problems without treatment. In N. Heather, W. Miller, & J. Greely (Eds.), *Self-control and the addictive* behaviors (pp. 198–242). New York, NY: Maxwell Macmillan.

Solomon, M. (2009). *AA-not the only way. Your one resource guide to 12 Step alternatives including a comprehensive directory of licensed professionals and treatment programs* (2nd ed.). Anchorage, AK: Capalo.

Volpicelli, J., & Szalavitz, M. (2000). *Recovery options: The complete guide: How you and your loved ones can understand and treat alcohol and other drug problems.* New York, NY: John S. Wiley.

c. History

Acker, C. (2002). *Creating the American junkie: Addiction research in the classic era of narcotic control.* Baltimore, MD: John Hopkins.

Berridge, V. (2004). Why alcohol is legal and other drugs are not. *History Today, 54,* 18–20.

Berridge, V., & Edwards, G. (1987). *Opium and the people: Opiate use in nineteenth century England.* New Haven, CT: Yale University Press.

Blumberg, L., & Pittman, W. (1991). *Beware the first drink! The Washington Temperance Movement and Alcoholics Anonymous.* Seattle, WA: Glen Abbey.

Bynum, W. (1968). Chronic alcoholism in the first half of the nineteenth century. *Bulletin of the History of Medicine, 42,* 160–185.

Cassedy, J. (1976). An early American hangover: The medical profession and temperance 1800–1860. *Bulletin of the History of Medicine, 50,* 405–413.

Courtwright, D. (1982). *Dark paradise: Opiate addiction in America before 1940.* Cambridge, MA: Cambridge University Press.

Ferentzy, P. (2001). From sin to disease: Differences and similarities between past and current conceptions of chronic drunkenness. *Contemporary Drug Problems, 28,* 363–390.

Herd, D. (1991). The paradox of temperance: Blacks and the alcohol question in nineteenth century America. In S. Barrows & R. Room

(Eds.), *Behavior and belief in modern history* (pp. 354-375). Berkeley: University of California.

Hickman, T. (2000). Drugs and race in American culture: Orientalism in the turn-of-the-century discourse of narcotic addiction. *American Studies, 41*, 71–91.

Jaffe, A. (1981). *Addiction reform in the progressive age: Scientific and social responses to drug dependence in the United States*. New York, NY: Arno Press.

Levine, H. (1978). The discovery of addiction: Changing conceptions of habitual drunkenness in America. *Journal of Studies on Alcohol, 39*, 143–174.

Lindesmith, A. (1965). *The addict and the law*. Bloomington: Indiana University Press.

Lindesmith, A. (1968). *Addiction and opiates*. Chicago, IL: Aldine.

McCormick, M. (1969). First representations of the gamma alcoholic in the English novel. *Quarterly Journal of Studies on Alcohol, 30*, 957–980.

Morgan, H. (1974). *Yesterday's addicts: American society and drug abuse: 1865–1920*. Norman: University of Oklahoma Press.

Morgan, H. (1981). *Drugs in America: A social history, 1800–1980*. Syracuse, NY: Syracuse University Press.

Musto, D. (1974). *The American disease: Origins of narcotic control*. New Haven, CT: Yale University Press.

Porter, R. (1987). *Mind forg'd manacles: A history of madness in England from the Restoration to the Regency*. Cambridge, MA: Harvard University Press.

Randall, S. (2010). Women and drug addiction: A historical perspective. *Journal of Addictive Diseases, 29*, 117–126.

Roizen, R. (1993). *Merging alcohol and illicit drugs: A brief commentary of the search for symbolic middle ground between licit and illicit psychoactive drugs*. Paper presented at the International Conference on Alcohol and Drug Treatment Systems Research, Toronto, Ontario, Canada, 18–22 October, 1993.

Roizen, R. (2004). How does the nation's "alcohol problem" change from era to era?: Stalking the social logic of problem-definition transformations since repeal. In S. Tracy & C. Acker (Eds.), *Altering American consciousness: The history of alcohol and drug use in the United States, 1800–2000* (pp. 61–87). Boston: University of Massachusetts Press.

Rorabaugh, J. (1979). *The Alcoholic republic: An American tradition, 1790–1840*. New York, NY: Oxford University Press.

Scull, A. (1993). *The most solitary of afflictions: Madness and society in Britain, 1700–1900*. New Haven and London: Yale University Press.

Valverde, M. (1998). *Diseases of the will: Alcohol and the dilemmas of freedom*. Cambridge, MA: Cambridge University Press.

White, W. (1998). *Slaying the dragon: The history of addiction treatment and recovery in America*. Bloomington, IN: Chestnut Health Systems/Lighthouse Institute.

d. Harm Reduction

DeBeck, K., Kerr, T., Bird, L., et al. (2011). Injection drug use cessation and use of North America's first medically supervised safer injecting facility. *Drug and Alcohol Dependence, 113(2-3)*, 172–176.

Dell, C., & Lyons, T. (2007). *Harm reduction policies and programs for persons of Aboriginal descent* (Harm reduction for special populations in Canada, No. 3). Ontario: Canadian Centre on Substance Abuse. Retrieved from http://www.ccsa.ca/2007%20CCSA%20Documents/ccsa-011515-2007.pdf

Des Jarlais, D., Wenston, J., Friedman, S., et al. (1992). Crack cocaine use in a cohort of methadone maintenance patients. *Journal of Substance Abuse Treatment, 8(4)*, 319–325.

Dolan, K., Kimber, J., Fry, C., et al. (2000). Drug consumption facilities in Europe and the establishment of supervised injection centres in Australia. *Drug and Alcohol Review, 19*, 337–346.

EMCDDA. (2010) Hedrich, D., Kerr, T., & Dubois-Arber, F. Drug consumption facilities in Europe and beyond. http://www.emcdda.europa.eu/attachements.cfm/att_101273_EN_emcdda-harm%20red-mon-ch11-web.pdf

Gillies M., Palmateer N., Hutchinson S., et al. (2010). The provision of non-needle/syringe drug injecting paraphernalia in the primary prevention of HCV among IDU: A systematic review. *BMC Public Health, 10,* 721.

Hathaway, A., & Tousaw, K. (2008). Harm reduction headway and continuing resistance: Insights from safe injection in the city of Vancouver. *International Journal of Drug Policy 19(1),* 11–16.

Kall, K., Hermansson, U., Amundsen, E., et al. (2007). The effectiveness of needle exchange programmes for HIV prevention—A critical review. *Journal of Global Drug Policy and Practice, 1*(3). http://www.globaldrugpolicy.org/print.php?var=1.3.1

Lee, H., & Zerai, A. (2010). Everyone deserves services no matter what: Defining success in harm-reduction-based substance user treatment. *Substance Use & Misuse, 45,* 2411–2427.

Lollis, C., Strothers, H., Chitwood, D., et al. (2000). Sex, drugs, and HIV: Does methadone maintenance reduce drug use and risky sexual behavior? *Journal of Behavioral Medicine, 23,* 545–557.

Marlatt, G. (2002). Highlights of harm reduction: Harm reduction: Pragmatic strategies for managing high-risk behaviors (p. 3). New York City: Guilford Press.

Palmateer, N., Kimber, J., Hickman, M., et al. (2010). Evidence for the effectiveness of sterile injecting equipment provision in preventing hepatitis C and human immunodeficiency virus transmission among injecting drug users: A review of reviews. *Addiction, 105,* 844–859.

Russell, S., & McVeigh, J. (2011). Next generation challenges: An overview of harm reduction 2010, IHRA's 21st conference. *International Journal of Drug Policy, 22,* 82–86.

Schwartz, R., Highfield, D., Jaffe, J., et al. (2006). A randomized controlled trial of interim methadone maintenance. *Archives of General Psychiatry, 63,* 102–109.

e. This & That

Alcoholics Anonymous World Services, Inc. (2001). Alcoholics Anonymous: The story of how many thousands of men and women have recovered from alcoholism (4th ed). New York, NY: Author.

American Psychiatric Association. (2000). *Diagnostic and statistical manual of mental disorders* (4th ed., text revision). Washington, DC: Author.

Atkinson, R., & Flint, J. (2001). Accessing hidden and hard-to-reach populations: Snowball research strategies. *Sociology at Surrey: Social Research Update, 33.* Retrieved from http://sru.soc.surrey.ac.uk/SRU33.html

Brown, I. (1997). A theoretical model of the behavioural addictions - Applied to offending. In J. Hodge, M. McMurran, & C. Hollin (Eds.), *Addicted to crime?* (pp. 13–65). Chichester, England: John Wiley.

Cepeda, A., & Valdez, A. (2010). Ethnographic strategies in the tracking and retention of street-recruited community-based samples of substance using hidden populations in longitudinal studies. *Substance Use & Misuse, 45,* 700–716.

Chueng, Y., Erickson, P., & Landau, T. (1991). Experience of crack use: Findings from a community-based sample in Toronto. *Journal of Drug Issues, 21,* 121–140.

Cochran, S., & Rabinowitz, F. (2000). *Men and depression: Clinical and empirical perspectives.* San Diego, CA: Academic Press.

Conway, K., Compton, W., Stinson, F., et al. (2006). Lifetime comorbidity of DSM-IV mood and anxiety disorders and specific drug use disorders: Results from the National Epidemiologic Survey on Alcohol and Related Conditions. *Journal of Clinical Psychiatry, 67,* 247–257.

Duncan, D. (1974). Drug abuse as a coping mechanism. *American Journal of Psychiatry, 131,* 724.

Erickson P., Butters J., McGillicuddy, P., et al. (2000). Crack and prostitution: Gender, myths, and experiences. *Journal of Drug Issues, 30,* 767–788.

Ferentzy, P. (2002). Foucault and addiction. *Telos, 125,* 167–191.

Ferentzy, P., Skinner, W., & Antze, P. (2010). The Serenity Prayer: Secularism and spirituality in Gamblers Anonymous. *Journal of Groups in Addiction & Recovery, 5,* 124–144.

Fischer, B. (2003). Doing good with a vengeance: A critical assessment of the effects and implications of Drug Treatment Courts. *Criminal Justice, 3,* 227–248.

Foucault, M. (1978). *The history of sexuality: Vol. 1. An introduction.* New York, NY: Vintage.

Foucault, M. (1979). *Discipline and punish: The birth of the prison.* New York, NY: Vintage.

Graham, L., Matthews, S., Dunbar J., et al. (2009). *The national drug related deaths database (Scotland) report.* Information Services Division, Scotland.

Griffiths, P., Gossop, M., Powis, B., et al. (1993). Reaching hidden populations of drug users by privileged access interviewers: Methodological and practical issues. *Addiction, 88,* 1617–1626.

Guarino, H., Deren, S., Mino, M., et al. (2010). Training drug treatment patients to conduct peer-based HIV outreach: An ethnographic perspective on peers' experiences. *Substance Use & Misuse, 45,* 414-436.

Haggard, H. (1944). Critique of the concept of the allergic nature of alcohol addiction. *Quarterly Journal of Studies on Alcohol, 5,* 233-241.

James, W. (2002). *The Varieties of religious experience: A study in human nature* (centenary ed.). New York, NY: Routledge.

Jung, C., & Pauli, W. (1955). *The Interpretation of nature and the psyche: Synchronicity: an acausal connecting principle.* New York, NY: Pantheon Books.

Khantzian, E. (1985). The self-medication hypothesis of addictive disorders: Focus on heroin and cocaine dependence. *American Journal of Psychiatry, 142,* 1259–1264.

Khantzian, E., Mack, J., & Schatzberg, A. (1974). Heroin use as an attempt to cope: Clinical observation. *American Journal of Psychiatry, 131,* 160–164.

Macdonald, S., Erickson, P., Wells, S., et al. (2008). Predicting violence among cocaine, cannabis, and alcohol treatment clients. *Addictive Behaviors, 33,* 201–205.

Mate, G. (2008). *In the realm of hungry ghosts: Close encounters with addiction.* Knopf Canada.

Nietzsche, F. (1996). *On the genealogy of morals.* New York, NY: Oxford University Press.

Nietzsche, F. (1998). *Beyond good and evil: Prelude to a philosophy of the future.* New York, NY: Oxford University Press.

O'Brien, C. (2006). What's in a word? Addiction versus dependence in DSM-V. *American Journal of Psychiatry, 163,* 764–765.

O'Brien, C. (2010). Addiction and dependence in DSM-V. *Addiction, 105,* xx–xx.

Orford, J. (2001). Addiction as excessive appetite. *Addiction, 96,* 15–31.

Peele, S., Buffe, C., & Brodsky, A. (2000). *Resisting 12 Step coercion: How to fight forced participation in AA, NA, or 12 Step treatment.* Tucson, AZ: See Sharp Press.

Penrod, J., Preston, D., Cain, R., et al. (2003). A discussion of chain referral as a method of sampling hard to reach populations. *Journal of Transcultural Nursing, 14,* 100–107.

Reinarman, C., & Levine, H. (Eds.). (1997). *Crack in America: Demon drugs and social justice.* Berkeley University of California Press.

Reynolds, C., 3rd, Frank, E., Perel, J., et al. (1999). Nortriptyline and interpersonal psychotherapy as maintenance therapies for recurrent major depression: A randomized controlled trial in patients older than 59 years. *Journal of the American Medical Association, 281,* 39–45.

Robinson, W., Risser, J., McGoy, S., et al. (2006). Recruiting injection drug users: A three-site comparison of results and experiences with respondent-driven and targeted sampling procedures. *Journal of Urban Health, 83,* i29–i38.

Rohan, K., Lindsey, K., Roecklein, K., et al. (2004). Cognitive-behavioral therapy, light therapy and their combination in treating seasonal affective disorder. *Journal of Affective Disorders, 80,* 273-283.

Room, R. (2003). The cultural framing of addiction. *Janus Head, 6,* 221–234.

Room. R. (2005). Stigma, social inequality and alcohol and drug use. *Drug and Alcohol Review, 24,* 143–155.

Salganik, M., & Heckathorn, D. (2004). Sampling and estimation in hidden populations using respondent-driven sampling. *Sociological Methodology, 34,* 193–239. doi:10.2307/3649374

Silkworth, W. (1937). Alcoholism as a manifestation of allergy. *Medical Record, 145,* 249–251.

Sussman, S., Lisha, N., & Griffiths, M. (2010). Prevalence of the addictions: A problem of the majority or the minority? *Evaluation and the Health Professions.* Advance online publication. doi: 10.1177/0163278710380124

Szalavitz, M. (2006). *Help at any cost: How the troubled-teen industry cons parents and hurts kids.* Washington, DC: Riverhead.

Szasz, T. (1974). *Ceremonial chemistry: The ritual persecution of drugs, addicts, and pushers.* Garden City, NY: Anchor Press.

Terplan, M., & Wright, T. (2011). The effects of cocaine and amphetamine use during pregnancy on the newborn: Myth versus reality. *Journal of Addictive Diseases, 30,* 1–5.

Watson, L., & Parke, A. (2009). The experience of recovery for female heroin addicts: An interpretive phenomenological analysis. *International Journal of Mental Health and Addiction.* Advance online publication. doi: 10.1007/s11469-009-9257-6

Werb, D., et al. (2011). Effect of drug law enforcement on drug market violence: A systematic review. *International Journal of Drug Policy,* 22(2), 87-94.

World Service Office, Inc. (1988). *Narcotics Anonymous.* Van Nuys, CA: Author.

Zinberg, N. (1984). Drug, *set, and setting: The case for controlled intoxicant use.* New Haven, CT: Yale University Press.